MW00785102

I have known Lou over 35 years when he bought and sold trains with my father Peter Bianco. I have learned a lot from Lou. He knows the hobby and calls it like he sees it. When he talks about the train hobby people listen.

~Kenny Bianco
Owner, Train World, Brooklyn New York

Lou's book is about the heart and soul of the hobby. What it's like to love toy trains. Lou writes from experience and with humor. Buy it, you'll learn and laugh.

~Tom McComas
Producer, TM Books & Video

From Lou to you: Train dealer, *Classic Toy Train* columnist and noted electric train raconteur Lou Palumbo shares his love of model trains, and his philosophy of the hobby.

~Bob Keller
Associate Editor *Classic Toy Trains Magazine*

This book is a great read.
I have known Lou for over 30 years and think the world of him. During my term as President of Eastern Division, TCA and later President of National TCA , Lou was (and continues to be) the co-chairman of activities and dealer in the largest hall we operate for our semi-annual train Meet in York, PA. Lou is on top of everything management and people-wise, he knows everyone very well and understands our fun hobby and how things are to be done right. His writings about the train hobby are spot-on, demonstrating his complete and thorough knowledge of train collecting and, most importantly, the people involved.

~Clem Clement.
Past President, Train Collectors Association

I NEVER MET A TRAIN
I DIDN'T LIKE

THE ART AND ENJOYMENT OF COLLECTING TOY TRAINS

I NEVER MET A TRAIN I DIDN'T LIKE
THE ART AND ENJOYMENT OF COLLECTING TOY TRAINS

Windy City Publishers
2118 Plum Grove Rd., #349
Rolling Meadows, IL 60008
www.windycitypublishers.com

Published in the United States of America

First Edition: 2014

ISBN:
978-1-935766-95-7

Library of Congress Control Number:
2013955846

PHOTO CREDITS
FRONT COVER: Lou at the Underground Railroad Shoppe
with a Lionel postwar no. 2343 Santa Fe F3 diesel locomotive.
Lou's pick for the most popular toy train of all time.
Photo by Dennis Brennan, *Classic Toy Trains* Magazine

BACK COVER: The Underground Railroad Shoppe caboose entrance.
Red Pennsylvania Railroad bay-window caboose with cupola.
Modeled from an American Flyer bay-window caboose,
and custom made into a clever entrance leading down to the shop.
Photo by Joe Stachler, TM Books & Video

I NEVER MET A TRAIN
I DIDN'T LIKE

THE ART AND ENJOYMENT OF COLLECTING TOY TRAINS

LOU PALUMBO

DEDICATION

To my wife Marcia, who has given endless encouragement,
help, and patience to a man who lives his hobby and loves being able
to share it with so many people.

To my father Frank Palumbo, who introduced me to the love of railroads,
both full-size and miniature, and taught me how to be an honest man.

To my mother Josephine Palumbo, who handed me beautiful wisdom
about people and said, "If you can't say anything good about a person…
make something up."

ACKNOWLEDGMENTS

Bill Brown, who opened the door for "Views From The Underground" with his publication, *Train Traders*, in 1987.

Tom McComas, who gave legs to "Views From The Underground" with a gracious invitation to write in his publication, *Toy Train Review Journal*.

The "Toy Train Revue" concept evolved into a printed magazine and my first column, "Views From The Underground," appeared in the inaugural issue, which was released in the summer of 1992. Tom remains a good friend, and I was happy to help him with his new venture.

Carl Swanson, editor of *Classic Toy Trains*, the number one O gauge magazine in the world! He worked with me to prepare much of the magazine material for this book, and for that I am very grateful.

Finally, my good friend and "toy train guru" Roger Carp, senior editor at *Classic Toy Trains*. Our regular phone meetings continually make my columns—and this book—entertaining and informative to train collectors everywhere.

Foreword

Lou Palumbo~
The ambassador for toy trains

By Roger Carp
Senior editor at *Classic Toy Trains* magazine

Writing the forward to this new book collecting the dozens of insightful and entertaining essays Lou Palumbo has written over the past two decades about the toy train hobby is quite an honor—and a huge challenge. What can I possibly say about the gentleman whom I consider the finest ambassador the leisure-time activity of collecting and operating toy electric trains could possibly have?

Truthfully, no one presents Lou with more color and enthusiasm than the man himself. Lou is unquestionably his own best representative. Therefore, anything I tell you about why everyone in the hobby loves and respects him will fall short of what he can tell you or that a visit to his fantastic store reveals.

All the same, I am thrilled to be asked to make the effort and explain to you what distinguishes Lou and sets him up as the perfect person to introduce toy trains or convey the passion so many thousands of individuals feel for the hobby.

Everyone Knows Lou

The hobby of toy trains has many terrific ambassadors—men and women who love vintage and contemporary models, build and operate layouts, and share their enjoyment with the public at shows and other public events. Some of these individuals belong to clubs or associations that collaborate to promote the hobby.

Still, when the editors of *Classic Toy Trains* magazine, members of the Train Collectors Association, or hobbyists in general talk about the most enthusiastic and best-informed ambassadors, they can't help but start with Lou.

How do folks know Lou? Some guys think of the excellent promotional and organizational work he does as an Orange Hall captain at the world-famous train shows put on twice each year in York, Pennsylvania, by the Eastern Division of TCA.

Other people know Lou as the proprietor of the Underground Railroad Shoppe, a train store in New Castle, Pennsylvania, an easy drive from Pittsburgh. Scale model railroaders and toy train fans can find everything they need for their layouts and collections there. Lou keeps his business open all year. During the holidays he invites visitors to see one of the most delightful O gauge layouts ever!

But what about the many thousands of devoted toy train hobbyists who have never attended the shows in York or stepped into the Underground Railroad Shoppe? How do so many of them know Lou and consider him a longtime friend?

Simple—nearly everyone involved in the toy train field has read and been informed and entertained by Lou's short and thought-provoking essays on the hobby. He publishes them under the title, "Views From The Underground."

These days, the carefully written columns appear in issues of *Classic Toy Trains* (and always to the satisfaction of regular readers of the magazine). Back in the 1990s, Lou submitted his insightful writings to TM Books & Video, which showcased them in different publications, notably price guides on Lionel trains.

Now, thanks to this brand-new book, you'll have the opportunity to read in a single source virtually every one of Lou's "Views From The Underground."

ADDING LOU TO *CLASSIC TOY TRAINS*

Lou was a familiar figure to me from the time I joined the staff of *Classic Toy Trains* in 1988 well into the first years of the 21st century. Attending the York shows and reading his articles for TM Books & Video enabled me to think of Lou as someone who was friendly, kind, and knowledgeable about old and new toy trains. We exchanged waves in the aisles of the Purple and then Orange Halls at York, where our booths were located, and even commented to each other via mail if one of us had read and liked something the other had written. Yet nothing more.

All of that changed in the early months of 2007. Lou proposed authoring a regular column for *Classic Toy Trains*, and the editorial staff discussed his offer.

Our magazine had never featured a single individual unaffiliated with Kalmbach Publishing Co. commenting on a consistent basis about the hobby. Yes, outsiders had written guest essays and shared their opinions on a host of topics. However, the idea of having one person do so in each issue had never come up.

We wondered whether Lou could possibly develop more than a dozen columns. Even if he could, we questioned whether our readers would respond favorably month after month to what Lou had to say. Still, it was worth the risk.

No surprise that Neil Besougloff, then the editor of *Classic Toy Trains*, asked me to serve as the magazine's liaison with Lou. I looked forward to the assignment and requested a list of potential topics from our nascent columnist.

I was impressed by how quickly Lou answered me and mailed a long group of ideas. The subjects, I could tell, were both serious and light—insightful perspectives on the entire hobby and humorous considerations of its members.

Next came a fat envelope filled with a batch of essays. "This is good," I told Neil. "Lou has taken everything seriously and already come through with columns we can publish." Clearly, any worries we might have had about not getting the material and having to pester Lou to write something to meet out deadlines had vanished. I felt confident our staff had picked a real winner.

IMPROVING THE MAGAZINE
Even better than receiving the columns, either typed on paper and mailed to me or submitted digitally as emails with attachments, were the telephone calls from Lou that followed each communication. Over the phone I learned more and more about this man, his love of toy trains and his dedication to his extended family and legions of friends, his lifelong hobby, and his noteworthy business.

More about all of that but first a plain statement of fact: Lou's columns have improved the contents of *Classic Toy Trains*. Without any bit of doubt.

What causes me to make such a bold and blanket claim? Because of Lou's central place in the hobby and the varied hats he wears, our magazine has been able to explore and discuss every possible area of interest regarding toy trains.

In the six years Lou has been writing "Views From The Underground" for *Classic Toy Trains*, he has shed light on every aspect of buying and selling, amassing and running, and appreciating vintage and contemporary trains. He has commented on the broad range of people who share the passions of operating and collecting those playthings. He has offered views on the prospects of the hobby, observing it from the viewpoints of manufacturers, retailers, and participants.

It comes as no surprise that many of the individuals making and selling toy trains today want to know what Lou is thinking. The same is true with the fellows who don't qualify as movers and shakers in the world of miniature trains, yet who love what they own and feel compelled to listen once Lou begins to talk.

JUST YOUR ORDINARY GUY
What is there about Lou that makes him an authority in the eyes of editors, manufacturers, retailers, and hobbyists? After spending hours on the phone with

him and sitting in front of my computer editing his columns, I think I may have figured out his appeal and significance. More than anyone else in the hobby, Lou beautifully blends the roles of ordinary guy loving trains and expert casting a smart and occasionally critical eye at what is going on at all levels of toy trains.

Ordinary? Okay, maybe "typical" is the better word to seize on when describing Lou. Ordinary leaves you thinking he is somehow run of the mill.

Lou is typical of the thousands of readers of *Classic Toy Trains* and the slightly past middle age guys hanging around train stores and hobby shops like the one he owns. Meaning, he received his first electric train as a youngster in the post-World War II period. In Lou's case, it was an American Flyer passenger set led by a steam engine and tender. Santa Claus brought it for Christmas of 1950.

The years that followed saw Lou treasuring the S gauge set and doing all he could to add to its roster. He helped his mom and dad whenever they asked and waited impatiently for a route delivering local newspapers, all to pick up a few dollars he could squirrel away for another freight car or section of track or even an accessory. Little by little, Lou recollected, his Gilbert two-rail empire grew.

Lou struck me as typical in other ways than his boyhood commitment to an electric train. His love of family was nurtured early on, as he assisted his father with odd jobs and chores and worked alongside him building an S gauge layout. Together, they made sure a miniature train ran for hours under the Christmas tree in the Palumbo household. In doing so, Lou and his dad were establishing a great tradition. Needless to say, the next generation in the big family has continued it.

One of the most typical things about Lou—and probably the trait I enjoy most about our friendship—is how he fell for rock 'n' roll as a teenager. Me too!

Lou loves to reminisce about his youthful days as a drummer in local combos as well as the high school band. He appreciates the terrific music that emerged in the late 1950s and early '60s. Everybody has his or her favorites, and Lou is no exception. Like many toy train enthusiasts, he expresses a particular love for doo-wop groups. Get him going on the subject, and he'll wax eloquently about Jimmy Beaumont and the Skyliners, the Del-Vikings, and the Vogues, all originating in Pittsburgh.

Typical as well is Lou's marrying not long after college and then starting a family. Marcia has been a loyal and loving "soul mate" since they met. Lou praises her as the rock of the family and the foundation of his life.

Today, Lou and Marcia delight in the accomplishments of their daughters Kelly, Michelle, and Melissa and son Todd, and their spouses, not to mention the 10 grandchildren.

Infatuated with O Gauge

Family life proved to be a blessing in every sense for Lou. He eagerly embraced fatherhood and gradually rose to become the patriarch of the extended clan, a role that fits him as comfortably as his highly coveted "Got Trains" sweatshirt. Having kids pulled Lou pulled back into the world of toy trains with the power of Magne-Traction. He wanted more of the trains and accessories that had captivated him during his early and adolescent years in the 1940s and '50s.

The solution, as other guys were discovering in the 1970s and '80s, was to place advertisements in local newspapers and search high and low for old train sets and individual models. The response was overwhelming, and Lou felt proud of the collection he assembled. Of course, he couldn't keep everything—and did not want to. Prewar items and many of the S gauge pieces had less appeal to him.

Lou did that for several years in the 1970s and into the next decade. That was about all he had time to do. Like so many of his peers, he also was raising a family and holding down a job. Upon graduation from college Lou was employed as a caseworker for the Pennsylvania Department of Welfare in the county where he resided. He served as executive director of that agency for 28 years prior to retirement. Trains were an avocation, and hardly more than that.

But keep in mind that Lou is a daring guy, one filled with enough energy and ideas to fill all his waking hours and a few more. Passionate about toy trains and eager to test the market, he decided in 1985 to open a store devoted to model railroading.

When Lou has a plan, you can count on him to have checked out every angle in advance. This is a guy who doesn't rush into something with haste or a lack of preparation. To the contrary, he examined what it would take to establish a successful store and how he could best meet the needs of a clientele fascinated with vintage models yet curious about the new trains being released by Lionel.

Initially, Lou worked evenings and weekends until he retired in 2004. Now, Lou is living a dream.

An Expert in His Right

Morning phone calls from Lou usually involve gabbing about preferred teams (Lou and I indulge loves for the Los Angeles Dodgers) and music (always another old-time singer or combo to rave about). Then we have to exchange the latest news about our kids—and in his case, grandchildren. That's followed by talk about buddies in the toy train hobby.

Shortly after, though, conversation switches to the column Lou is crafting or an idea I want to toss out for his consideration. These are the moments when I quit thinking of Lou as ordinary or typical, just another guy who loves his trains. More and more, I realize how unique he is, an expert unlike anyone else I know.

You see, every person who has spent more than five minutes with new or old trains has opinions about the state of the hobby, its glorious past, and its tenuous future. "Here's what I think should be manufactured" and "I just can't believe someone hasn't done this" echo throughout the aisles of train meets in every state of the Union. No one has ever accused train enthusiasts of being quiet or boring.

Nonetheless, only Lou has, as far as I am aware, lifted himself from the sprawling ranks of those spouting opinions to arrange his thoughts in a coherent manner in short and often brilliant essays. Additionally, he has been doing this on an ongoing basis for nearly all of the past 20 years. That, let me tell you, is tough!

PICK YOUR SUBJECT

In other words, Lou has been at the forefront of thinking about toy trains in the United States since the collecting side of the hobby peaked in the 1980s and '90s. He has been to the mountaintop and looked out to survey what lies below. Ever since then, he has assessed changes and set out to explain why he believes times continue to be good. Never pessimistic or cynical, he wants others to take part in the love fest he has for model trains and value them as warmly as he does.

Not a facet of the hobby exists that Lou has failed to investigate and write about with intelligence and foresight. As readers of this anthology of his columns will discover, he has thought long and hard about the marketplace and the people currently selling and buying antique and new O and S gauge replicas.

Similarly, Lou has scrutinized the principal manufacturers, evaluating what they produce and how they are advertise their new additions. Of particular importance are the stores like his that reach out to newcomers to promote the hobby. He wants to make sure they are doing what they can to satisfy customers.

Lou wisely never forgets to have fun. His columns occasionally poke jabs (never with bitterness or cruelty) at fellow hobbyists. Targets of his good-natured humor include partisans of American Flyer, hoarders of boxes, and those shifty-eyed "investors" determined to accrue a fortune through their toy trains.

From one essay to the next, what you'll be rewarded with varies. Lou may put forth in one column a novel perspective on the relationship between Lionel and MTH Electric Trains, a view likely to spark hours of contemplation and then heated remarks at the next train show. Turn the page and you may end up smiling as he recounts building a layout at home with his father more than half a century in the past. You'll soon be recalling the model railroads you designed and made.

Incisive commentary and warm nostalgia fill Lou's many essays. So do insights into how to manage a train store and get along sweetly with the crustiest of customers. Can't leave out his ideas about why guys love trains, cars, and rock.

A VISIT TO LOU'S

Perhaps the best manner of ascertaining the success of this book is waiting to see how many readers conclude that they simply must make a pilgrimage to the Underground Railroad Shoppe. They'll cruise into New Castle and head for the shortened replica of a red-painted caboose that serves as the façade. After parking, they will enter the rear of that railcar and head downstairs to the store's main area.

Lou deliberately put the shop beneath the brick building dominating the block. That structure was erected in 1898. After serving as an elementary school (Marcia Palumbo was a student there), it was refurbished during the New Deal.

Sharp-eyed visitors never miss noticing that the entire structure, including the professional offices and music studio above the store, is named for Frank A. Palumbo. Could it be? You're right! Lou owns the structure and made sure to name it in honor of his father for having introduced him to electric trains.

That devotion to previous generations exemplifies the respect Lou feels for his past. He talks about how his father and mother climbed the economic ladder in America and how his grandparents and parents immigrated here from southern Italy. They came with determination to succeed; now Lou and their other kids and grandchildren have proved what thrift, industry, and ingenuity can do.

Rather than keep describing the Underground Railroad Shoppe, let's just accept Lou's invitation to drop by and explore the store. You can count on finding this gentleman sitting behind the main counter, greeting customers (both adults and children) and stepping out to see how he can answer questions and offer help:

Walk around the spacious yet crowded aisles of the Underground Railroad Shoppe, and you may think that you have traveled back to an earlier time. One of Lou's goals was to have his customers feel as though they were in a train store or hobby shop from their youth back in the 1950s or '60s. He wanted the atmosphere to be friendly and easy-going—no pressure to buy something or rush in and out.

The Finest Layout

Before wrapping up this appreciation of the ambassador of toy trains, it's essential to shift the spotlight from Lou's past and the dozens of columns he has written to the finest O gauge model railroad he has ever planned and constructed. Once again, I consider him both ordinary and rather amazing in this key regard.

Typical in that Lou has been building layouts his entire life and lauds them as absolutely crucial for anyone claiming to love the hobby. He comes right out and declares that trains are meant to be operated—and not just on loops of track assembled only during the holidays and put under the limbs of a Christmas tree.

Yet the size and complexity of the multiple-level 16 x 28-foot O gauge extravaganza visitors to the Underground Railroad Shoppe can admire from November to January raise Lou high above his comrades. He is an expert when it comes to developing a smooth-running model railroad complete with 14 trains running and operating accessories of all kinds as well as an enormous array of illuminated structures.

Don't worry about the layout being an exhibit fit more for a museum than a train store. Never imagine children will feel left out when they see the railroad.

Lou wouldn't be himself if he erected a layout appealing only to the most dedicated hobbyists, the rare breed insisting on extremely realistic scenery and digital age technology. To be honest, Lou knows all about what aficionados refer to as "hi-rail modeling" and "command control." Let a customer pose even the most detailed question about those fields, and he can frame an appropriate answer.

To Lou's credit, he created an O gauge railroad that, frankly, looks a lot like what most of his customers would do if they had the available space at home, the resources, and the time. Scenes can be crowded, with plenty of three-rail track filling central areas and competing for attention with the little trucks and buses on boulevards. Signals of every type border the main lines, and figures stand nearby.

Invite children to come inside the store and they dash to the backroom, where Lou has built the massive layout. They stare at it the way he and millions of his peers gazed at displays in department stores and other commercial outlets during the postwar era. Trains captivate them, and they compete to yell out about the locomotives racing toward them or the cool details they've suddenly noticed.

Whimsy is the name of the game at the Underground Railroad Shoppe. Realism should never be overlooked, states Lou, but having fun and entertaining dominate his cast of mind when it comes to electric trains. They always have, he announces, and they always will. And you wonder why Lou paraphrases the great American humorist Will Rogers by saying, "I never met a train I didn't like."

Taking Your Time

"Take your time"—Lou gives that handy bit of advice to folks visiting his store and feeling overwhelmed by the array of vintage Lionel and American Flyer models neatly displayed or engrossed in studying the brand-new MTH, Williams, and Atlas engines lined up on shelves and in glass cases. "Take your time," Lou tells newcomers and longtime customers. "No need to rush once you're here."

The same words apply to anyone strolling along a corridor to reach the back room where the layout holds court. There is so much to take in that hurrying will be a big mistake. Haunted houses, grand passenger depots, flashing signs and lights, oil refineries and steel mills, an amusement park with many operating rides and a roller coaster, a sprawling used-car lot, a towering mountain, and what Lou calls "Palumbo Country Club golf course"— his O gauge extravaganza practically screams out to be enjoyed by everyone who loves miniature railroading.

Lastly, taking your time is the best recommendation I can pass along to readers of this book. Relax and browse here and there to glean the gems of Lou's thinking about the wonderful hobby of toy trains. Why barrel through this group of essays when you can spend hour after hour gaining insights, remembering special trains, and revisiting the golden age of electric trains after World War II?

Before closing and inviting you to jump into the pearls of Lou's lifetime of hobby knowledge, let me offer a bold prediction. As much as I guarantee you will learn from these essays and assuredly chuckle and nod with approval, I am certain something better will occur as you read. You will feel affection for the man who writes "Views From The Underground." In no time at all, you're likely to consider Lou a friend, a trusted pal to share conversation and a cold beverage.

Then you will understand why those of us in the hobby who already feel fortunate and honored to call Lou a friend put him in the rare category of being an ambassador of toy trains. No one represents this great hobby with more dignity, knowledge, solid and balanced judgment, warmth, and good cheer than he does.

The Underground Railroad Shoppe is located at
1906 Wilmington Road
New Castle, PA 16105

To learn more about the store and its inventory or
to find out the dates and times the O gauge layout can be visited,
please contact Lou Palumbo and his staff at 724-652-4912,
or go to www.undergroundrrshop.com

INTRODUCTION

It seems like I started to write this book 25 years ago.

In 1987, my good friend, Bill Brown, asked me to write a column for his new toy train hobby newsletter, *Train Traders*. Bill, who also lived in New Castle, Pa., knew I was actively buying and selling vintage and new toy trains, so I would be able to share insights and opinions more informed than a typical hobbyist. I decided to call my column "Views From The Underground" and intended to share my views of the current train market and collector activity.

More people ended up reading "Views From The Underground" than just my friends and a handful of toy train enthusiasts because in the early 1990s Tom McComas, who owns and manages TM Books & Video, requested that I write a column in his new periodical, *Toy Train Review*. Later, he turned to me to provide "Views From The Underground" articles for many of the price guides for American Flyer, Lionel, and MTH Electric Trains he published in that era.

In the earliest "Views From The Underground" I always analyzed the pulse of the toy train market. I also described current trends in the hobby and offered recommendations about new train production. The articles were quite candid, and many of my suggestions eventually came into fruition in future productions.

Around that time I started to use the logo of a pair of eyes looking out of a partially opened manhole cover. This image was meant to give the idea that we, at the Underground Railroad Shoppe, knew more than anyone about toy trains.

This collection of "Views From The Underground" will serve as a guide for any new toy train enthusiast who plans to collect toy trains as a hobby. It gives a great overview of the hobby as I have observed it from the inside over the past 25 years.

The book also serves as an easy reference to many of the enjoyable articles that I wrote exclusively for *Classic Toy Trains* magazine, the premier and most widely circulated publication in the hobby. You'll find plenty of homespun humor included in articles that are as entertaining as they are informative.

Of course, as my regular readers know, I use the phrase "Keep Searchin' as the ending tag line for every column. The reason is simple. I once wrote that toy train collectors remind me in the best sense of fifth graders going on a scavenger hunt. If you notice the expression on the faces of the guys as they walk around a train show or first walk into a train store, you'll see the excitement and anticipation of a great "find."

I refer to them as fifth graders because that time of life impressed me as an age of innocence, when nothing else was on your mind but what you were searching for. Collectors all but revert to that time of life when they search for a new item for their train world.

This wonderful feeling and sense of carefree enthusiasm capture the essence of my book. It includes many stories related to these times of collecting enjoyment and also reminiscent of days gone by, when all was good with the world and we were all kids.

Enjoy the book and always ...

Keep Searchin'

Lou and his dad at a mall train show in Cleveland, Ohio, 1984.

CONTENTS

2007

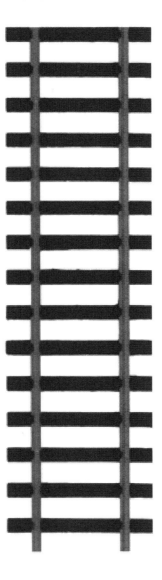

Price Guides and Selling Your Trains

This, the initial "Views from the Underground," should be clipped and saved as it will be a collector's item in years to come. I'll be writing this column in every issue of Classic Toy Trains until I run out of ideas or just get tired of sharing my pearls of wisdom related to toy trains.

In each column I plan to give you information about the toy train market, old and new products, manufacturers, dealers, and any other oddities about the hobby.

Who am I?

I have been a train buff all of my life. My dad worked on the Pennsylvania RR, and he started me in trains (real ones and toy). I grew up in New Castle, a small western Pennsylvania town, with three older sisters, so I was the prince!

I went to school in the 1950s, graduated from college in the '60s, worked 38 years for the Pennsylvania Department of Welfare, and retired in 2004.

I married my lovely high school sweetheart Marcia 40 years ago, and we have a son, 3 daughters, and 10 grandchildren to show for it. I've been collecting, buying, and selling trains for most of my life and own and manage the Underground Railroad Shoppe here in New Castle.

"Views from the Underground" is not new. You may recognize the name from articles in past price guides. Now, I think price guides should be titled "This is What Your Trains Used to be Worth."

Seriously, it's hard to write an accurate price guide these days. I know they are only meant to be "guides," but many collectors put a lot of stock in these books.

I still use price guides, but with reservations. The price range of each item has expanded. Back in 2000, a Lionel postwar Santa Fe F3 A-A combination in excellent condition was worth between $500 and $600. Now those same F3s are going for anywhere from $250 to $650, depending on who is buying and selling. The market is very loose. Good deals are out there for buyers as well as sellers.

I divide the year into two parts. October starts "train season," which builds up in November and December. January and February are for working on your layout.

Things slow down in March, and by April most everything is completed for "train season." I guess you could say it all starts with the show that the Eastern Division of the Train Collectors Association puts on in York, Pa., every October, and it ends with the April York show.

The summer months—May, June, July, August, and September—are usually reserved for other recreational activities. Folks spend their money on vacations, but the ardent collectors still search for new finds at flea markets, summer train shows, and train shops they visit while out of town.

One of the questions that I frequently get asked is, "When is the best time to sell my collection?" My answer is always: "Never!"

I usually follow that with, "Why did you buy them in the first place?" If you bought them to sell, then you probably could have done a lot better buying the right stocks in the stock market.

I never want to sell my trains. Still, there were times during the years I was collecting that I had to sell some of my collection to pay for my children's weddings and college educations.

So that's the answer. Sell your trains only when you absolutely have to. Otherwise, let your heirs divide them up after you're gone. I have a few favorites I instructed my kids to bury with me!

These are just a few of my "Views from the Underground." If you have any thoughts you'd like to share, drop me an email at trainplum@yahoo.com.

Any entertaining items and questions or ideas are welcome. I want to make this column enjoyable and informative.

Keep searchin'!

NEW BLOOD IN AN OLD HOBBY

I've been collecting and selling toy trains for more than 30 years. I've watched preschool-age kids come into my Underground Railroad Shoppe in New Castle, Pa., with their parents. Now I see some of these same kids bringing their own children to see the trains. I guess time does fly when you're having fun.

O and S gauge toy trains are a great family tradition, especially around the holidays. I think we will have toy trains as long as there is the Christmas season. However, the outlook for the train collecting hobby is another story.

The hobby was reborn in the early 1970s just about the time that middle-age baby boomers started to collect the trains they had as kids in the 1950s. You know what happened then. Over the next 30 years there has been a great desire among these men to own toy trains.

New manufacturing companies, such as MTH Electric Trains and Williams Reproductions, were formed. Hobby clubs, led by the Train Collectors Association and the Toy Train Operating Society, were overrun with members. The train market was great!

To keep this market alive it needs new blood. Many of the older collectors have gone, and more are sure to follow. Some of their collections are being sold, so plenty of vintage trains are available.

Meanwhile, Lionel, MTH, and other manufacturers keep on churning out new products for the market. It seems like the law of supply and demand is working against the collecting hobby.

Two good things have happened to help the industry. First is Thomas the Tank Engine. This character, featured in books and television programs, is responsible for developing thousands and thousands of new train lovers.

The award-winning *Thomas the Tank Engine & Friends* series of videos has introduced many children to trains. These are kids who would never have been exposed to the love of trains. They start with the wooden trains, get a starter set, and become train enthusiasts at a young age. A "really useful engine" indeed!

Another shot in the arm was given to the toy train hobby by the popular movie, *The Polar Express*. Lionel seized the moment on this one. It made a great O gauge replica of the train that was in the movie, and it became the all-time best-selling train set in Lionel history, beating the Blue Comet, the Scout, and everything in between. The Lionel Polar Express set is still going strong and will be good as long as the movie remains a favorite for every holiday season.

Other companies are bringing out commercial trains to entice collectors into the hobby. MTH is doing a great job with its sports team trains, as well as the new Coors Silver Bullet set.

I see another development in my store. Baby boomers are now grandparents. Many of them are building train layouts for their grandkids in their homes. Papa is spending some of his retirement money to make a nice train layout in his house so that the grandkids can have something to play with when they visit. This way grandma won't object to some of their nest egg being spent at the train shop.

Television appearances by toy trains also benefit our hobby. Poor Bobby Bacala of *The Sopranos* never got to run his O gauge Blue Comet, but the whack job at the train store on that HBO series reached more people than any toy train advertisement in history.

All of us who admire Joshua Lionel Cowen and A.C. Gilbert, toy train promoters of the past, owe thanks to David Chase. He's the creator of *The Sopranos*.

Keep searchin'!

2008

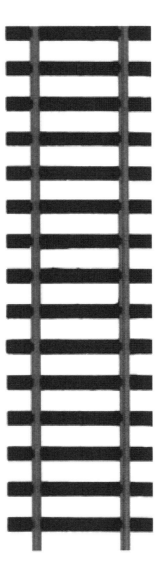

FOR THE LOVE OF TRAINS

I have been a train lover for as long as I can remember. My dad introduced me to full-size trains before I was in school, and I got my first electric toy train when I was in first grade. The love affair has been going on ever since those days in the late 1940s.

Steam trains were my first favorites, and I can remember some of the big ones that traveled near our family's home. Soon, though, I came to love the great F3 "covered wagons" that were popular in the 1950s.

I would travel to Chicago from Pennsylvania each summer to visit my sister. My dad, who worked for the Pennsylvania RR, would get free rides for himself and his family, so that was our mode of transportation to the Windy City.

I can still remember the thrill I'd get when I would see that yellow light glowing off in the distance as our passenger train to Chicago would approach the station where we were waiting at 2:00 a.m. The diesel horn could hardly be heard at first. The platform would then begin to shake and finally explode in a seemingly unbearable noise as those huge F3 diesel units would pass us by pulling the beautiful streamlined coaches that soon would stop in front of us so we could board.

Our family would get on the majestic Pullman coach amid the sleeping passengers. Soon, we would be falling sleep to the rhythmic clicking of the wheels riding on the rails headed for "Chi Town." We awoke in the early morning seeing quiet Indiana farmlands and smelling the wonderful aroma of ham and eggs coming from the dining car.

While eating breakfast, we passed the steel mills of Gary, Indiana, and then we began to see the Chicago skyline. We finally arrived at Union Station, which was filled with as much railroadiana as my eyes could handle.

It was in this station that I first saw the Santa Fe *Super Chief* with its glorious red, yellow, and silver F3 A-B-A diesel locomotives ready to pull a long train of streamlined passenger cars to the West Coast. What a sight!

If you saw the *Super Chief* or any of its streamlined brothers and sisters on the Santa Fe, you know exactly why this was the most popular toy train. Visions of that train filled my young mind and made me want to relive all of this magic in miniature.

The toy train companies must have known all this because Lionel had its Santa Fe F3 units while the smaller American Flyer line featured Alco PA diesels painted in that railroad's warbonnet scheme. O gauge and S gauge hobbyists could couple models of streamlined passenger cars behind those locomotives and have their own version of the *Chief* or the *El Capitan*.

Keep in mind, though, that I grew up in the Keystone State and my dad worked for the Pennsylvania RR. Good as the Santa Fe might have been, I wanted something decorated for the Pennsy.

During my childhood in the 1950s, I would wait each year for the new Lionel and Flyer catalogs and search for a replica of a Pennsy diesel. I really wanted Lionel to paint one of its F3s in Tuscan Red. Never happened. Not until 1979 did Lionel produce my dream diesels.

Layouts were the best way to enjoy toy trains. Kids and dads spent hours re-creating the world around them. Then kids would stand by the tracks and dream about the great places "iron ponies" were taking the passengers as the trains rumbled by. The passengers would look out the windows and see a warmly lit farmhouse on a snowy night and wish they were home. These are the things that we re-created on our layouts.

The romance of trains was powerful to everyone during my childhood days. I figure that's why those same kids, 50 years later, are still reliving their youth through toy trains. Because we know those days will never come again.

Keep searchin'!

New Blood for Williams

Whether you were attending toy train shows or participating in Internet chat groups, the big topic has been the purchase of Williams Electric Trains by Bachmann Industries. I've been doing a lot of thinking about this and can't help but feel a bit sad about the change yet hopeful for our hobby.

As the owner of a train store who regularly goes to train shows, I've watched the toy train market roller coaster up and down for the past 30 years.

Back in the 1970s and early '80s, we were happy to be able to buy some of our old favorites, remade by the new owners of Lionel. In the years that followed, other companies were formed, adding to the new collecting phenomenon. K-Line, Williams, Weaver, and Mike's Train House (now MTH Electric Trains) joined the parade to meet the needs of this rapidly expanding group that had money to spend.

During the 1980s and '90s, tons of O gauge product were sold to collectors and operators. Competition was fierce. Each company was trying to get a large share of the market by bringing out new and improved designs and promising electronic features that were nice and expensive.

From my perspective, one firm really seemed to get it. They understood the market and what hobbyists truly wanted. Williams consistently put out a very good product for a modest price. Its locomotives might not have the elaborate sounds that the others did, but they could be trusted to have a great sounding horn or whistle and a bell.

Williams offered a large selection of die-cast steamers and diesels with great paint jobs. They remade many of the postwar classics and added a lot of new and current road names. In addition, the motors and reversing units on these locomotives were reliable and inexpensive to repair. No engine sold for more than $500, with most ranging from $150 to $250.

All this and only one catalog a year. It wasn't difficult to sell this product to a new consumer when it was stacked up against the other guys. They (the other guys) should take notice and put their own "Williams-like" trains in their new lines.

I'm holding my breath about what the future holds for the new Williams by Bachmann line. I hope Bachmann will continue the Williams tradition and, based on what I've seen it do over the past few years, find ways to make this O gauge line even better.

Frankly, I believe this infusion of new blood for Williams can do it and benefit the toy train hobby!

When I look at Bachmann's history, I find that it has continued to raise the quality of its Large scale products. It is right up there with the big guys. You can now buy a three-truck Shay steam engine and tender with DCC sounds and other sophisticated features.

The same trend of making constant improvements while keeping the price line steady has been true of the HO and N scale trains Bachmann has released. Of course, when you talk about Bachmann, most of us think of Plasticville. Those buildings are in my hall of fame of O gauge collecting.

With the Williams line, we'll have to wait and see what Bachmann does. My main hope is that it will maintain the high standards Jerry Williams set for his trains. I'd hate to see Williams products in discount stores, hanging on pegboards in impossible-to-open hard-plastic shrink-wrapped packaging.

I hope Bachmann understands the unique place Williams trains have. There's no reason to use them to compete with other manufacturers by adding high-priced sounds and features. Bachmann should do what it can to help the modestly priced, reliable, and respected Williams locomotives keep their reputation.

Really, the best advice I can give Bachmann is to build on the Williams tradition and be sure any improved features don't cause prices to skyrocket. Then this new blood will help the hobby.

Keep searchin'!

WHAT'S THE REAL VALUE OF YOUR TRAINS?

What's happened to the market for O gauge steam locomotives? The early 1980s seemed to be the heyday for buying and selling all those beautiful and powerful postwar Lionel steam engines and tenders, complete with die-cast boilers, puffing smoke, shrill whistles, blazing headlights, and shining marker jewels.

As the owner of the Underground Railroad Shoppe, a hobby shop located in New Castle, Pa., I bought dozens of used Lionel steamers in the '80s. The no. 773 Hudson, particularly the version cataloged in 1950, was the most desirable of these workhorses, followed by the striking no. 746 Norfolk & Western J, which was cataloged from 1957 through 1960.

But every top-of-the-line steam locomotive was in demand from collectors as well as operators. The nos. 726 and 736 Berkshires were high on hobbyists' lists. So were small Hudsons, including the nos. 646, 2056, and 2065 from the 1950s.

Looking back, I could not keep any Lionel steamers in my shop during the Christmas season. They flew off the shelves like Santa's sleigh pulled by reindeer across the sky on the night of December 24.

Now these locomotives are all sold on occasion, but they are not the hot sellers they once were, even at reduced prices from days gone by. What's happened to change the scene and make hobbyists turn their backs on the classic postwar steamers?

The market has been flooded with new die-cast steam engines from Lionel, MTH, and Williams. Their list of features is long, and you can get sound-equipped models for less than $250. For better or worse, these locomotives have largely killed the postwar market. However, if you have a like-new to mint postwar steamer in its original box you still should get premium dollar for it.

Personally, I like the old postwar steamers. They have that nostalgic value, and I can repair them without spending a lot of money on failed electronic parts.

In the meantime, are you like me and wondering why MTH and Lionel put out so many large catalogs every year? The two toy train giants must spend a fortune preparing these gems because they are really well done. Still, I think it's a huge waste of money and paper.

One good catalog each year should be plenty to show the new products. Sometimes less is more. It looks like MTH and Lionel are flooding the market with new products, but I may be wrong.

The orange-and-blue Lionel boxes are by far the most recognizable in the hobby. I see this in my store when new customers shop for their first train. MTH has made a dent and really does put pressure on Lionel to keep up with the hobby. Together, they make better trains than we ever had back in the 1950s. The new technology has really changed the hobby.

As I mentioned in my column in the February issue of CTT, Williams carved out a unique place for itself in the new market with its remakes of postwar locomotives and cars. These items did not have all the new electronics, but dollar-for-dollar they were second to none for a good, operating train. Bachmann will do its best to carry on that tradition.

What's my advice? Don't buy new trains and expect them to skyrocket in value. After checking the recent price guides, I did not see many of the trains produced in the past 10 years going up in value. Just buy trains old or new that you like and enjoy them. That's their value.

Keep searchin'!

Toy Train Shows Built the Hobby

Train shows have done a lot to promote the hobby over the past 40 years. Whether they're put on by individuals or collecting groups, shows are always enjoyable and can introduce you to the best trains.

Before I opened the Underground Railroad Shoppe in 1985, I sold trains at many shows. My buddy Gary Zippie and I did 28 of them in one year back in the early 1980s (that's more than two shows every month). Our bags were always packed.

As I said in an interview: "I'm a devout Catholic and go to church on Sundays…unless there's a train show."

Most of the trains I sold were used prewar and postwar Lionel and Flyer. I did shows in school gyms, church halls, hotel ballrooms, union halls, German clubs, and farm show buildings—wherever tables could be set up to display trains.

Many of the sites were not easy places to load and unload boxes filled with trains. High steps, slippery ramps, and rumpled carpets were a few of the problems. Still, we persevered.

Mall shows were very popular in those days. I often traveled many miles to attend the shows, setting up on Friday afternoon and knowing that I would be working until Sunday night. Those were long weekends, but also profitable ones!

For my money, the meets that are put on by the Eastern Division of the Train Collectors Association in York, Pa., every April and October are the very best in the world. A friend asked me the other day if the most recent show had been a good one. He had heard some people say it was and others reply that it was not.

My evaluation of a show—from a dealer's standpoint—represents only one view. And it's right to the point: If the people were there and your items didn't sell, you have to adjust your prices. York shows always have more than 10,000 people attending, so if you're not selling it's your fault.

While I still enjoy going to the local train shows, I don't sell at many of them these days. The main reasons for this change is that attendance is down and costs keep going up. Hotel and table costs have risen, as has the price of gasoline, which affects the overall cost of doing a show. When I go, it's usually just for the fun of seeing friends and keeping a finger on the pulse of the market.

Internet auction sites, especially eBay, have put a crunch on local shows. Thanks to the Internet, people have a way to buy trains without leaving home. Although I sell over the Internet, I don't think the experience is the same as going to a hobby shop or a show and getting what you want.

Of course, buyers must be alert when they purchase anything at a show or over the Internet. Many of the trains brought to my shop for repair have been purchased over the Internet or at a show and were not properly tested first. They come to us to be fixed.

Always try to buy from a dealer or an eBay site you know, someone who will stand behind the sale. The electronic components used in today's trains are expensive to repair, and trains will not run without them.

I made many friends at the train shows that I did over the years. We had somewhat of a fraternity and looked forward to every show. We had regular customers that would look for us at every show. Those days are gone, but I'm glad I was there.

Now my shop has helped me make the same kind of friendships with many people over the years. I like to say that we are lucky to be in the toy train hobby. It's like living in a fantasy land.

Keep searchin'!

Forty Bid, Forty Bid a Fifty-Dollar Bill

Some of my earliest memories involve going to local auctions with my folks. Auctions were exciting, thanks to the rhythmic chatter of the auctioneer and the thrill of the winning bid.

I learned a lot at those auctions, especially as I studied the faces of participants. There were the same feelings of excitement I felt at important athletic contests. After all, much of the psychology of an auction is based on elevating the emotions of buyers.

Another reason I liked to go to auctions was that I would get a toy or something neat. One time my dad bought a large metal airplane that I could almost ride. I don't know what happened to that plane and sure wish I had it now!

Auctions are still wonderful parts of my life. Naturally, the ones that I find most interesting to attend are those selling collectible toy trains.

If you go to a toy train auction, you'll benefit from following a few of the "rules" I've picked up over the years. They'll help you get good buys and avoid being burned.

First, inspect the items as much as you can before the auction. You can save yourself an unwanted surprise when you take it home. Most auctions are as-is purchases.

Second, always set a maximum price in your head before you bid. People tend to get into bidding wars over an item that extends beyond the price in their comfort zone.

Third, be certain to include the buyer's premium (usually 10 to 15 percent) and the state sales tax when you figure your maximum bid.

After inspecting the items that I'm most interested in bidding on, I look for a good place to sit. For a lot of toy train enthusiasts, that means a chair near the front of the auction. Not me. My preferred seats tend to be near the back of the hall.

Why? Since I own a retail shop I may end up competing against my regular customers at local auctions. I really hate doing that, so by staying in back I can check out who the interested parties are and avoid bidding against any of my friends or customers.

Whenever I attend national train auctions that are held live in conjunction with eBay, I consider it a dealer auction. Then it's every man for himself!

These auctions can be brutal, and the action is fast and furious. You better be on your toes when bidding because bidders who don't pay attention make mistakes. Most of my errors have been on items I did not buy. I blinked and missed the item.

When attending an auction, leave your ego at home! How often have I watched the bidding get out of hand when two people try to show how tough they are.

All it takes are two "auction challenged" people to run up the bids until an item is sold at a ridiculous price. I can remember once watching two foolish guys bid up a Lionel Rico Station that had been glued together. It sold for a whopping $125.

Later, in the same auction, a second station (sealed in its original box) sold for $30 to the guy who didn't get the first one. Needless to say, this brought a rousing cheer from the crowd!

I think that auctions will be on the increase in the years to come, due to the number of train collections that will be for sale. So, it would be a good idea for you to become an expert auction buyer. Remember, this takes practice and a lot of discipline. Luckily, if you miss one train, there's always another one coming.

Keep searchin'!

DAY-OLD DOUGHNUTS
Blowout Sales May Not be Good for the Hobby

When I was a kid back in the 1950s, one of my favorite things was spending the couple dollars that I received for Christmas at the "Day-After-Christmas Train Sales" held by most of the stores that carried toy trains. Traditionally, all Lionel, American Flyer, and Marx trains and accessories were 50 percent off on the day after Christmas.

This sale was a one-day event because most of the items were cleared out that same day. Merchants would take what was left and put them away for the next year.

In those days, everyone who had a storefront (besides department stores) carried electric trains. Drugstores, hardware stores, tire stores, appliance shops, confectionery shops, and even some gasoline filling stations sold trains. I guess Lionel wasn't picky about who offered its trains.

Merchants usually ordered trains after the American Toy Fair was held each February. The trains were then built and shipped throughout the year to be sold at the holidays. The merchants would then pay Lionel.

The markup tended to be double the cost. However, any train merchandise that was not sold during the shopping season was usually sold at cost the day after Christmas.

In January, the cycle would start again. However, the real train shops did not do this. They were usually year-round hobby shops and so gave only small discounts after Christmas since they couldn't afford to sell a lot of trains at cost.

Today's train market is different. Now trains are bought and sold all year, with manufacturers offering large sales—sometimes 80 or even 90 percent off retail at any time during the year.

These "blowout" sales result when manufacturers overproduce and must sell items below wholesale to move their excess inventory. I think that mass blowout sales weaken the entire train market and may ultimately destroy it.

All of this reminds me of a conversation that I once had with a friend who owned a very profitable bakery. I asked him why he didn't sell day-old goods like other bakeries. He replied that he gave his day-old baked goods to the Salvation Army and the local homeless shelter.

The key, my friend went on, was to project his daily baking to what would be sold. He had tried selling day-old doughnuts at half-price, but found that his normal sales fell because customers waited for day-old goods instead of buying regular-priced products.

Large amounts of train products sold at blowout prices may spell doom for the train industry. Even though these sales are great for consumers in the hobby, they devalue any notion of collectibility as well as investment stability of the trains already owned by those consumers.

People will wait for the mass blowout sales, and profits will decrease for the manufacturers and their distributors. This is the main reason I think it would be better for them to make less product and carry over those items that don't sell.

No surprise that consumers like blowout sales. Even so, they need to remember that things are worth only what you pay for them. Companies should make profits so they continue making the trains that we all can enjoy in this hobby.

Half-priced, next-day pastry may taste just as good as fresh. But did you ever notice that small bakeries are all but gone from today's business landscape? Maybe they sold too many "day-old doughnuts"!

Keep searchin'!

THE COLLECTING OF TOY TRAINS...PRICELESS
You Can't Put a Value on the Friends You Make

How do you determine the value of the toy train hobby in your life? Do you add up the worth of your locomotives and cars as given in the latest pocket price guides? Do you figure out how much you've spent on the track and transformers used on your layout? Or do you focus on the intangibles that give you pleasure?

I started thinking about these questions after talking with a longtime friend at a train show. Over a 30-year period, he had put together one of the finest and most complete collections of postwar trains that I'd ever seen.

My friend did not develop this collection by himself. No, he did it with a bunch of fellow hobbyists who traveled the train show circuit together. Wherever I set up my tables, that group of friends was sure to show up. They would be some of the first customers, searching for new additions to their personal collections.

These guys traveled in a pack like wolves. That's a compliment! Although they competed fiercely with each other to get something unique for their collections, the immense enjoyment they took in finding a special model and admiring what the others had found, was obvious.

My friend and his pals spent hours preparing for each show—much like hunters prepare for deer or pheasant season. They went over their wish lists, checked them against reference books, and looked over what they owned.

They would meet before the train show, and some of them would drive there together. After the show they would gather to display what they had picked up for overall group evaluations. Those days were priceless to them.

Then, little by little, I saw the group grow smaller. Curious, I asked my friend what was happening. The answer he gave me fit the others in the gang.

My buddy had sold nearly all of his collection. "For very good money," he added proudly. He gave the money to his kids, and it helped them with the needs of their own families. "Nothing wrong with that," he said, and I agreed.

But my friend said that he still loved toy trains and wanted to "get back into the hobby," but he wasn't sure how to go about it. Besides, he worried that things would never be the same as they had been.

Much of the fun for him and his pals was being in that "pack." You can't reproduce those memories because that's what they are— "memories."

Every time one of those guys would look at his collection, he didn't just see an individual piece or calculate its value. He saw the good times spent obtaining it and recalled the great stories, meals shared, jokes told.

When my buddy sold his collection for all that money, he ripped a big hole in his heart, which is why I felt bad for him. He had lost something that was priceless. Now he was sure he had lost something that he couldn't get back.

Happily, the story does not end there. I ran into my friend last year, and he was wearing a smile. An acquaintance had given him some trains to sell. First, my friend was cleaning and repairing those models—and was having a great time. He was going to shows again and meeting new collectors.

"My interest has been renewed," my buddy said, "and I'm thinking about starting another train collection. I found some new guys to go to the shows with."

I guess the fever never dies. As long as there are trains to acquire, display, and run—and people to share them with—we can enjoy this great hobby.

Keep searchin'!

MASTER OF YOUR DOMAIN
Building Layouts Has Always Been Part of Our Hobby

In the early years of our hobby, kids played with Standard gauge trains on the floors of their living rooms. I envision the Lionel Blue Comet and State Sets rolling over the hardwood floors of mansions, with an assortment of prewar stations, tunnels, and other accessories scattered throughout the house as these beauties rumbled by. I guess you could say these were the first layouts.

During the postwar years, many more kids were introduced to O and S gauge trains. Sets from Lionel, Gilbert, and Marx exploded across America. By the 1950s every kid had one.

However, due to the size of houses in the postwar era, there seldom were extra rooms to build large layouts. Most kids put their trains around a Christmas tree and created their own little world within the circle of track that defined the boundary of their domain.

If kids were lucky, they might receive a 4 x 8 sheet of plywood that they placed in a corner of the small basements in the homes of those days. A guy had everything if he had two separate rail lines—one for freight and one for passenger. He really had it all if he owned a Santa Fe passenger set and a Berkshire or Northern freight set, a pair of switches, and a big transformer.

Today, of course, O and S gauge layouts far surpass anything was made in the prewar or postwar years. Take a look at a typical issue of Classic Toy Trains and you'll see wonderful layouts that are the expression of the creativity, planning, and hard work of the hobbyists who built them.

Layouts can be very sophisticated. New electronics enable the locomotives made by major manufacturers to act and sound just like the real ones. Command control lets you operate your railroad in ways that no one could have predicted two or three generations ago.

Meanwhile, new cottage industries have sprouted up that make everything imaginable so you can add realism to an O or S gauge model railroad. Guys and women, too, are always tweaking their layouts to put on one more structure, road, mountain, or piece of track to enhance their world.

Why not? This is where hobbyists escape from the real world. No crime, no drugs, no foreclosures, no politics, no wars, and no taxes in this perfect world. You can't beat that!

The technology and equipment on today's layouts are light-years ahead of what was available in the early years of trains. It's like comparing rotary dial telephones with our cell phones, blackberries, or camera phones. Like something out of science fiction!

The only thing that is the same is the feeling you get when you work on your miniature empire. It doesn't matter how large or how fancy a layout may be, the builder still gets a feeling of being the creator of his or her world.

People often bring pictures of their "masterpieces" to my hobby shop in Pennsylvania. They show off their layouts and proudly point out items that they've purchased from our store.

I'm pleased to see fathers and children, husbands and wives enjoying this hobby together. I always tell folks, "I never met a layout I didn't like." There's something magical about every toy train layout. I really believe they represent the bloodline of our hobby.

I've never completed the layout in my store. I'm always looking to change or improve it. The fun is looking for new ideas and discovering new products. It's only in this world that I am in complete control. You can't ask for anything better than to be the master of your domain.

Keep searchin'

CIRCLE THE WAGONS
Now's the Time to Find New Ways to Enjoy Your Trains

It hit me when I pulled up to the dock to launch my boat this summer. The dock was only about half-filled where usually 70 to 80 boats were tied up.

I was told that many spots were not being filled this year. In the past there had always been a waiting list for these prized spaces along this beautiful lake.

Where my family and I relax isn't the only place that has experienced a decline in business. The same downward trend has affected other hobbies, especially those that involve collectibles, such as baseball cards, comic books, and toys.

"It's the economy, 'buddy!'" (I don't like to use the word "stupid"). That's the phrase that can explain the state of what I call the "fun industries."

I see some of the same things happening in our hobby. Attendance has decreased at train shows. The rising cost of gas has a lot to do with that. Dealers are complaining about poor sales. Auction prices are falling.

Prices will always decrease when there is less buying going on. The supply side is being inflated with more used trains being sold by people who are feeling the crunch of the falling economy. Guys are willing to take a loss to generate some cash. There are some dealers dumping product on the market just to pay daily operating costs.

This is actually a great time to buy trains *if* you have extra dough. This part of the hobby industry will return because it flows with the country's economy.

If you were collecting toy trains during the "dot com" years of the 1990s, you may recall how record sale prices were set. Everybody seemed to have money. I could not keep trains on the shelf of my hobby shop. That has certainly changed now.

So what do we do? Until the economy recovers—and it will, trust me—let's enjoy the trains that we already have. Don't abandon this hobby; just find new ways to have fun with it.

One suggestion is to tear down all or part of your O or S gauge layout and rebuild it with some major changes in mind. Add a mountain, make a river, or develop a railroad yard. If that sounds too big, focus on detailing one area.

Another possibility is to trade trains with your buddies. It's fun and costs nothing. You can operate a new locomotive or try out an accessory without spending any money. Even better, your friendships with fellow hobbyists grow stronger and you all enjoy the hobby more.

Instead of missing train shows, how about carpooling with some buddies? That saves gas and allows for good conversations to and from train meets.

A fourth idea is to start collecting toy train paper. I'm talking about old catalogs, ads, and other memorabilia. The prices are reasonable and you'll learn a lot about trains.

How about restoring some of your junkers? You can buy beat-up models for a song and have fun getting them to run or redecorating them. Start by repainting a few tank cars—they're easy to do and look good when finished!

Keep the hobby alive by using what you have. Toy trains have carved a strong place in American life and will stand as a great hobby for many years. We're fortunate to be in a hobby that lets us use the items we collect. We all have shelves, boxes, and closets full of collectible gems. They operate and so provide hours of enjoyment.

John Wayne used to circle the wagon train to defend it from attack. It provided time for the cavalry to arrive and save the day in the movies. Then they all rode off into the sunset.

The toy train hobby will always be there. Trains will come back the way the economy will. Now's the perfect time to broaden your interests and have more fun. That way, trains will continue to provide wholesome entertainment for generations to come.

Keep searchin'!

2009

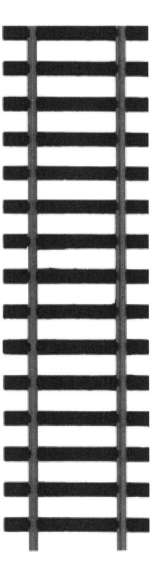

Anatomy of a Column
22 Years of Thinking from "The Underground"

Thousands of toy train enthusiasts will be picking up this issue of Classic Toy Trains to broaden their enjoyment of this hobby. Some are reading this magazine for the first time; more have been with CTT since it began publishing in the fall of 1987.

You may wonder what's the story behind "Views From The Underground," the exclusive column that I write for CTT. Here's some background plus ideas about how you can make it better.

The first incarnation of "Views From The Underground" appeared in 1987 in *Train Traders Magazine*, a newsletter published by Bill Brown. It next showed up as a column for *Toy Train Review*, which Tom McComas put out in the 1990s. I also wrote it as a supplement for Tom's guides on Flyer, Lionel, and MTH.

For the past year or so, "Views From The Underground" has returned to print as a regular column in CTT. As you can guess, I'm glad to be back writing about two of the things that I love most in life—collecting and operating new and old toy trains.

"Views From The Underground" is what the title implies: my views based on the experience I get buying, selling, and trading toy trains. The Underground Railroad Shoppe, which I own and manage, is where I get a lot of my information.

Most of you have probably figured out why I gave the column its name, even if you've never stepped into my store. In the past 30 years,

I've made many friends in this hobby. I still rely on their input to gather material to share in the columns.

Stories are told at gatherings of collectors. I try to get as much information as possible so all points of view are represented in each article. It's not hard to get guys talking about their experiences in the hobby. Meeting people at train shows is also a good source for information and new material. I used to get many letters from collectors and operators, but that has now been replaced by emails. They help me gauge the impact of my columns, so please keep them coming!

Phone conversations with other dealers supply me with more information and insights into the current hobby scene. They enable me to get a perspective from sellers about the pulse of the hobby. They see a lot of things that manufacturers should be doing to augment the hobby. I like to be constructive when offering any criticism. Many of the dealers are vocal and don't hesitate to offer their thoughts.

I gather all of this information and write a column each month that's informative and entertaining. I try to blend nostalgia with news about toy trains as they are today. We hobbyists like to reminisce about the "good old days" yet still enjoy the hobby as it is now.

As you can guess, I like to interject many of my personal experiences into "Views From The Underground" as well as my own opinions (which sometimes get toned down by the CTT staff). I also like to sprinkle in a little humor to keep things entertaining.

Despite all of my hard work and experience, I would never claim that I write this column on my own. Without you, the readers of CTT, the stories just wouldn't get told. Simply put, I need your input to have new material to share with the readers.

So please write or telephone the Underground Railroad Shoppe (1906 Wilmington Rd., New Castle, PA 16105; 724-652-4912). Or feel free to send me an email at trainplum@yahoo.com

Let me know what you think is going on in the hobby today, and where you think collecting and operating toy trains is headed in the future. Tell me about the best trains on the market now – and the worst ones. Which manufacturers put out great products? What do you like to read about in my column and in CTT as a whole?

Keep searchin'!

The Day the Music Died
Collecting Modern-Era Trains Changed with Reissues

Fifty years have gone by since the airplane crash in Iowa that killed rock 'n' roll singers Buddy Holly, Richie Valens, and the "Big Bopper" on a cold night in February of 1959. Years later, singer-songwriter Don McLean penned American Pie to recall that sad time, which he called "the day the music died."

We know music lived after that day, but the song referred to a day when the music world got a real hard kick in the gut that took time to get over.

The toy train hobby experienced a similar kick in the gut that I believe changed our approach to collecting. In fact, it's something that we're still dealing with.

What I'm talking about dates from the 1970s, when General Mills leased the rights to produce and market Lionel trains. General Mills manufactured trains through a subsidiary known as Model Products Corp., and we refer to those trains as "MPC."

Initially, MPC trains were inexpensive and unimpressive. Each year, however, they improved in design and operation. The trains got better as train collecting exploded. By the end of the '70s, MPC was putting out a traditional line and a collector line. The two distinct product lines encouraged operating as well as collecting O gauge trains.

The collector trains were basically locomotives made with postwar tooling and having several new paint schemes. Guys loved these different F3s, Train Masters, and Geeps.

Each year people looked forward to the new collector items being produced. The MPC catalogs were not very big; many guys bought two of each locomotive, one to run and one to collect. They could because many of these models sold for less than $100.

With prices so low and the quantities made so limited, many of these engines and sets sold out in a few months. And their value skyrocketed. The unnumbered *Blue Comet* set went from $125 in 1978 to $500 in 1982, and the no. 8262 unpowered Southern Pacific F3 B unit climbed from $119 in 1982 to $1,000 in two years!

More prewar and postwar trains came out of the woodwork in the '80s. Trains were all over the place—so were the guys treating them like investments. The growth was fast and unnatural. I don't know if it was good for the hobby, but it sure was fun. That's why I consider the 1980s the golden years of train collecting.

Then, under the leadership of Richard Kughn in 1991, Lionel Trains Inc. cataloged the no. 18007 Southern Pacific 4-8-4 GS2 *Daylight*. Other than having different headlights, this steam locomotive was identical to the no. 8307 Southern Pacific GS4 that MPC had cataloged in 1983. That model originally sold for $400, but its value increased in five years until examples were going for $1,500 to $2,000.

The release of the 18007 caused the value of the 8307 to plummet. The latest edition of the annual *Greenberg Pocket Price Guide to Lionel Trains* lists its value at $560 in new condition.

For many collectors the release of the Southern Pacific GS2 *Daylight* represents the moment when Lionel lost its credibility related to producing collector trains. Until 1991, hobbyists had assumed that once Lionel produced a locomotive, it would not reissue that model. But now collectors no longer felt confident about paying a high price for an item that might be reissued again and again.

It seems that Lionel just gave in to requests from people who refused to pay the inflated rate of the 8307 GS4. In toy train collecting, the release of the 18007 was "the day the music died."

Keep searchin'

RUNNERS AND JUNKERS
The Growing Impact of New "Old" Trains

I was really glad to see the latest Lionel catalog, with the news about the introduction of the Postwar Conventional Classics. This series features reissues of several desirable O gauge train sets as well as individual locomotives and cars that were brought out during the postwar era.

Besides looking very nice and running smoothly, the first entries in the Postwar Conventional Classics series have reasonable prices. Lionel likely did this to compete with the Golden Memories series that is being put out by Williams by Bachmann. Those O gauge trains have gained popularity with hobbyists, who win as more legitimate reissues appear.

Before Lionel and Williams started bringing out these products, there was an enormous market for locomotives known as "runners." These models from the prewar and postwar eras weren't like-new or mint, but mechanically they were fine.

Folks who built O gauge layouts to operate trains used runners with confidence. Collectors also liked runners because they made it possible to avoid operating like-new or mint items, whose condition and value would decline after many hours of running.

The presence of reissues of postwar trains from Lionel and Williams has affected the place of runners in the hobby. The value of trains in very good to fair condition has decreased drastically since these remakes appeared.

Take the Lionel no. 2321 Lackawanna Fairbanks-Morse Train Master diesel (first cataloged in 1954). Until recently, a 2321 with a maroon roof in very good to excellent condition was valued at $500 to $700. Today, it goes for $200 to $300. In addition, the gap between excellent and like-new has widened.

The new "old" trains from Lionel and Williams have had a similar impact on "junkers." Those vintage trains in fair to good condition, often missing some original parts, can be restored to look new.

Professionals with years of experience did many of these restorations. These guys were extremely talented, and their work was widely respected in the toy train world. Other restorations were the work of hobbyists who just enjoyed the challenge and fun of searching for the right parts and then repainting and relettering their old trains.

I'm afraid reissues of postwar trains will put an end to that restoring. It's not worth all the cost and effort when you can buy a new "old" locomotive for a reasonable price. Williams and Lionel have struck a hard blow to the restoration business.

Let's go back to our example of the Lackawanna F-M Train Master. Both Lionel and Williams by Bachmann have introduced reissues that look as nice as the original and run better. The Lionel maroon-roof FM is priced below $240, and the Williams model goes for $10 less.

Hobbyists who have $250 to spend on a runner have three real choices. They can opt for an original 2321 in very good condition, a restored junker, or a brand-new reissue. All three locomotives will run well, and none has much collectible value.

I like the new Lionel and Williams by Bachmann reissues and feel confident that I'll sell many of them in my train store. Of course, I know restoration artists and don't want to see them go out of business. So I'd consider their services if you own a vintage locomotive. You'll have something that was made in America and brought up to date right here in the U.S.A.

Of course, if you have the talent and the time, I think it's even better to fix up a junker. The feeling of accomplishment you'll get is priceless—and that's what makes our hobby so great.

Keep searchin'!

OPTIONS AND OPPORTUNITIES
Modern Trains Sound and Operate Great…
and That Can Be a Problem

Recently, I spoke with my good friend Kenny Bianco, the owner of Trainland in Long Island, N.Y. I've known Kenny for more than 30 years, from when he was working for his dad, Pete Bianco, of Train World in Brooklyn, N.Y.

For those of you who don't recognize the name, the late Pete Bianco was one of the pioneers in toy train retailing after the resurgence of the collecting hobby in the 1970s. Pete was one of the truly good guys in our hobby, and I really miss him.

Kenny and I were talking about the problems we see while managing our stores and talking with customers. We agreed that the biggest problem in the toy train hobby today is the expense related to repairing the electronics components that operate the new trains in today's O gauge market.

Today's trains sound and operate better than their predecessors, and that includes the finest locomotives developed by Lionel during the postwar era. They can do more and enable operators to assemble sophisticated trains.

The problem lies in the expense and availability of replacement parts when new locomotives fail. Models equipped with state-of-the-art command control systems can be very expensive to fix.

Most of the time those locomotives don't run at all when circuit boards malfunction. Customers are left with models purchased for $300 to $1,400 that now need a board or two that costs $150 to $300, not counting installation fees.

Don't forget that most models have a one-year warranty. Repairs to locomotives older than that are usually the responsibility of their owners.

We need options that are reasonable. I'm issuing a challenge to you electronics geniuses out there. Market a universal reversing unit and sound system for less than $60 that the average repair-person will find easy to install. There are a lot of really nice locomotives out there that need a reasonably priced fix.

People like Kenny and me have been repairing E-units, whistles, and horns for years in prewar and postwar trains. They are still running today. It's too bad we can't say the same for some of the new stuff.

But this means a great opportunity exists. A guy might make a lot of money by coming up with those parts. Remember, I said "reasonable" and "easy to install."

Before signing off for this issue, I want to add a postscript to my "Day the Music Died" piece in the February issue of *Classic Toy Trains*. That article sparked some spirited responses from collectors and operators.

I've always favored operating toy trains over just collecting them. But the column looked back at the 1980s, when collectors poured millions of dollars into the hobby and made it what it is today. For that I am thankful. And in those days, many hobbyists were both collectors and operators.

I'm aware of the reissues of postwar trains in the 1980s. However when Lionel brought back the no. 8307 Southern Pacific *Daylight* GS4 steam locomotive as the no. 18007 GS2 in 1991, it represented the first reissue of a modern-era engine that had greatly increased in value. It was the early 1990s when prices started to decline on modern-era Lionel trains. The collecting fever was over.

Thanks to everyone who took the time to write in.

Keep searchin'!

FLYER GUYS
I Love S Gauge Enthusiasts, But They are Different!

I recently attended a toy train auction organized by Stout Auctions. While there, I was reminded why I've always thought that American Flyer S gauge collectors make up a different breed from other toy train enthusiasts.

Let me preface my comments by saying that I consider myself an American Flyer collector. My first train, which I still have, was a no. 290 passenger set. In addition, over the past 25 to 30 years I've put together a very nice S gauge collection. So I'm not a stranger to the world of A.C. Gilbert and American Flyer.

However, I am not a pure Flyer guy. I also collect some prewar and postwar Lionel pieces, not to mention Marx trains. I call myself a "hybrid collector," and that designation suits me just fine.

Ever notice how defensive Flyer guys get when you mention Lionel, the three-rail king? Their hearts were broken when Lionel bought the American Flyer tooling and began putting out new S gauge trains as part of its line. Most Flyer guys acknowledge only those models made by Gilbert between 1946 and 1966.

Speaking of A.C. Gilbert, the auction that I attended in February of this year was very interesting. It featured furniture and personal contents from the office of the founder and president of the toy manufacturer with his name.

Some of the items auctioned included Mr. Gilbert's desk and a painting from 1913 that showed kids playing with what looked to be an Erector set. There was a set of William and Mary chairs, along with examples of original engineering art and company posters. The painting brought a show-stopping $22,000.

After I walked into the auction and hung my Lionel jacket on the back of one of the chairs being sold, a few Flyer guys admonished me. I actually thought the chair started to rumble when the Lionel logo covered its back. Maybe that was Mr. Gilbert's ghost protesting almost 60 years after his death. I quickly removed the jacket!

Lionel enthusiasts tend to tolerate Flyer guys. Too bad the opposite generally isn't the case!

Flyer guys never fail to express their dislike of Lionel's "unrealistic" three-rail O gauge track and non-scale trains. I guess the war of which gauge and brand is better, started long ago when everyone was young, has yet to end.

Sorry guys, but Lionel won that contest by sheer numbers. Of course, I've learned first-hand you'll never convince a Flyer guy of that.

Personally, I agree that S gauge is more realistic than O gauge. A set of sleek American Flyer Alco diesels looks great. They look even better when they're pulling the streamlined passenger cars that go so well with them.

You can't beat the looks of an American Flyer no. 336 Union Pacific 4-8-4 steamer pulling a set of heavyweight cars. The overall scale of S gauge trains and accessories fits well on a layout. I like to think that S gauge is HO on steroids!

Even so, experience has taught me that Lionel trains operate a lot better than their S gauge counterparts. Those O gauge models are sturdier and more colorful than Flyer's. Nothing Gilbert cataloged compared with Lionel's striking GG1 electric-profile engine or its massive Fairbanks-Morse Train Master diesel.

In fact, Lionel offered the greatest selection of diesels in the postwar era: Alcos, F3s, GP7s and GP9s, NW2s, plus the 44-tonners and the Train Masters. Its different steam locomotives proved to be more durable and featured a better whistle. Don't forget the 275-watt ZW, the best transformer ever made.

So you see, I still can't make up my mind between Lionel O gauge and American Flyer S gauge. Flyer guys need not worry – I still love all toy trains!

Keep searchin'

School Daze
Teaching Old Dogs New Tricks About Toy Trains

It really seemed funny to be sitting in a classroom again late this spring. It's been a long time since I had to listen to a lecture and take notes in order to prepare for a written and practical exam.

What was I doing back in school? Well, Lionel LLC's service department has undertaken a project geared toward restructuring the entire repair service division of the company.

One key aspect of this path-breaking program included a three-day intensive training course of diagnosis and repair of the new electronic components in the TrainMaster Command Control (TMCC) and Legacy trains.

This course is the first of four sessions Lionel has scheduled. They're open to every authorized service station.

My shop in New Castle, Pa., has been an authorized service station since 1985. Yet we've never been offered this type of training.

Like most repair personnel working in their homes or hobby shops, I've taught myself how to repair and maintain toy trains and accessories. My "education" involved reading manuals, doing thousands of repairs, and working with some talented repair people over the past 24 years.

To be honest with you, I feel that, as a repairman, I'm in the twilight of a mediocre career. But that's okay—my Underground Railroad Shoppe has some great guys working there. Together, we've made a lot of folks happy by giving new life to their trains.

Anyway, I was thrilled to get an opportunity to receive some good hands-on training offered by Lionel.

The class was run by Mike Reagan, who is the director of Lionel's customer service department. I've known Mike for quite a while, and he is hard to beat when it comes to knowing about toy train electronics.

The class ran from 8 a.m. to 8 p.m. for three days during the first week of June. Mike did a great job as our teacher. The instruction lasted for two days, and it was intense but with enough levity to keep us all relaxed. The third day was reserved for the testing.

It was really nice to see a lot of my friends in the class, and I have to say that there was a wealth of talent there.

Many good ideas were shared in the class, but I could tell that the material was new to a lot of guys. Seeing that the average age of attendees was around 60 made me realize that we ought to start looking for apprentices. The business of repairing and maintaining toy trains is going to be wide open.

Mike directed most of the training toward the diagnosis and repair of electronic components that are related to operating Lionel locomotives.

New manuals were made available, and new testing devices were introduced. The intense training emphasized the proper diagnosis of an electronic problem.

All of this training should work out to benefit you, our customers and the buyers of Lionel trains. It should, to start, lower the costs of repairs.

In addition, the new test fixtures will save a lot of time. Time saved will also reduce the total repair cost.

The restructuring of Lionel's repair services includes better online access to parts and better support regarding repair information. This move has been needed for a long time. There are also plans to streamline the parts replacement method as well as the reimbursement for warranty work done at the service stations.

Like everyone attending, I want to say thanks to Mike Reagan and Lionel for taking this step so that we can all have more fun in this wonderful hobby.

By the way, I passed both tests given on the third day and graduated "magna cum lousy" in my class!

Keep searchin'!

Italian Fantasy
Thinking About Toy Trains Very Far From Home

The reason most model train enthusiasts enjoy the hobby is that it is an extension of their ongoing romance with real trains. Railroads once circled this country like so many ribbons on a beautiful gift package.

Most of all, our memories of passenger trains remind us of an era that was good. We relate to passenger trains because they were the main model of transportation used in the United States at one time.

Every town had a train station that was part of a network throughout the land. This is the period of time that many of us build in miniature with our model railroad layouts.

Recently, my wife and I took a once-in-a-lifetime, 15-day tour of Italy. It was a wonderful trip around the entire country, by bus. However, we decided to leave the main tour for a day to visit some of my relatives in another province.

Our one-day excursion turned out to be the best time of the entire tour. My wife and I took a 300-mile train trip from Sorrento to Naples and then to a small town in the province of Caserta.

This day-trip provided a unique experience in reliving the days when the entire U.S.A. was connected by trains. During the excursion, two things went through my mind: how everything I was seeing would translate to a model train layout and why can't we have this type of train service in America.

The stations varied from large, modern terminals with many trains coming and going to small, rural stations with only two tracks in front of them. They were all clean and beautifully constructed. The track seemed to be in great shape as the ride was smooth.

Sometimes the electric-powered train ran at, what seemed to me, a very high speed. When it began to accelerate to top speed I felt the way I do when a jet airplane is taking off. It was really exciting to me, but did not seem to faze the regular travelers.

The best part of the ride was the scenery. Mountains, tunnels, bridges, vineyards, farms, waterfalls, and seaports were all a part of our one-day trip to visit the small town of my ancestors.

The views were spectacular when we traveled over the bridges that span scenic gorges. There are many tunnels cutting through the mountain range that divides Italy. Many towns are perched on these mountains; they were built on these high points for protection many centuries ago.

Lying between the mountains in the center of the country and both seacoasts is beautiful farmland. The farms are a picture-perfect tapestry of vineyards and olive and lemon orchards. Ideas for a toy train layout are endless.

It's easy to forget that trains run through some of the most picturesque parts of any country. We miss those areas driving on the crazy freeways—always cluttered with huge trailer trucks and noisy motor coaches that you wish weren't there. It is a lot better to sit back and enjoy the scenery.

The entire trip, both ways, cost less than $30 for my wife and me. And there was none of the stress that comes with a similar trip on our own highways. No reservations needed; if you miss one train, another will soon be coming.

I couldn't stop thinking that a great stimulus plan would be to rebuild our railroads so our country had a real nationwide transportation system that everyone could afford to use and enjoy. Not to mention the millions of jobs that it would create.

My trip to the "old country" was one of the highlights of my life. Yet I was able to relate it to the model railroad hobby because we are always looking for new ideas for our "fantasy world."

Keep searchin'

WILLIE, MICKEY, AND THE TRAINS
Kids Had All They Wanted With
Baseball and Trains in the 1950s

One of my favorite activities during my youth was going to a Sunday doubleheader baseball game in Cleveland. Major league teams played doubleheaders almost every Sunday then and on holidays like Memorial Day, the Fourth of July, and Labor Day.

The men's association at our church put together an excursion for fathers and sons. This included mass and a procession to the station, where we boarded a train going right to the stadium to watch a Cleveland Indians and New York Yankees doubleheader.

Everybody boarded the special train in New Castle, Pa., and it would arrive on a line that was next to Municipal Stadium. I loved the train ride as much as I loved the baseball games.

Steam locomotives pulled our trains in the early years. Sleek, modern diesels later replaced those engines. We traveled in coaches, with windows wide open because there was no air conditioning. You had to be careful not to stick your head out of the windows because cinders from the locomotive were always flying back.

Lunch was served in the baggage car along the way. And not a meal ordered off a menu. No, I'm talking about fresh ham sandwiches packed in waxed paper bags and bottles of ice cold soda pop buried in tubs of ice.

Trains were a big part of life. When I was a kid and baseball had yet to expand far beyond the Mississippi River, trains transported all the teams to their games.

I've always felt that baseball in the 1950s was the best that's ever been played. For the first time all the best players were permitted to participate. Jackie Robinson opened that door in 1947! Also, there were only eight teams in each league. The game had yet to be watered down with all the expansion teams created in the 1960s and '70s.

Baseball was pure. No drug-enhanced phonies making millions of dollars were playing. Every ballpark was different, which made games really interesting to the visitors.

Three of the greatest center fielders played in the same city at the same time. Willie Mays, Mickey Mantle, and Duke Snider played in New York for the Giants, Yankees, and Dodgers, respectively. Of course, baseball could be just as good outside New York. Future hall-of-famers showed up nearly everywhere. Players in the postwar era felt a special pride in the game that their modern-day counterparts seldom show.

The period I'm talking about as the greatest in baseball history was also a golden age of toy trains. Lionel and American Flyer were producing the best selection of toy trains, and these marvels were sold to more people than ever. Colorful catalogs, new diesel locomotives, and novel accessories kept amazing us, thanks to the Gilbert, Lionel, and Marx companies.

Now you can figure out why my O gauge layout includes a model of Ebbets Field, where the Brooklyn Dodgers played. I put it right alongside a railroad line. After all, two of my favorite things in life—right after my family and friends—are trains and baseball.

In the summer baby boomers had baseball, and in the winter it was model trains. We had all we wanted with these two great interests.

There was a good connection between kids and their fathers that's often missing today.

We were lucky to have grown up then and carry those memories to the hobby today. By the way, the 1950s was also the time when rock 'n' roll music changed the world, usually by way of 45-rpm records, which were introduced then. But that's another story for another day.

Keep searchin'!

DESPERATE TRAIN WIVES
Support From Your Spouse Makes the Hobby Better

I always feel good when I see a guy and his wife shopping for trains together. It's a good thing when spouses let each other enjoy their respective hobbies. When a husband and wife each have a hobby that they enjoy, it's really great when they get support from their "other half."

I'm no Dr. Phil, but I have to believe that mutual respect for each other's interest is good for a marriage. Besides, it makes shopping for the holidays and special occasions very easy.

Sometimes even the wife is a toy train collector. That seems to be the best of all worlds. I really enjoy those type of customers. I think, "This guy *really* has it made." Also, it's good for business at my train store!

Needless to say these perfect conditions are not always the case between husbands, wives and trains. In fact, I've seen cases where the train budget is not always approved by the Secretary of Treasury (the wife). Then she ends up acting like she's the Secretary of War!

Guys love to hide money so they can buy that favorite piece for their collection. I have seen many multi-folded $100 bills creep out of that secret compartment in guys' wallets, all so they can make that special purchase. Many guys have asked me to make sure all the price tags were off the trains before I pack them for the trip home. You'd think that wives would have caught on to those old tricks by now.

Back in the day when smoking was more tolerated, I used to have a occasional cigar in the rear office of my shop. The cigar smoke would make its way out into the showroom, and sometimes it would overpower the cedar smell of the smoke coming out of a steam locomotive.

One customer told me that I would have to stop smoking my cigars because the smell gave away the fact that he was making unscheduled stops at "that train store." Three years ago I quit smoking, but more to preserve my health than to preserve his marriage!

Over the years that I've owned the Underground Railroad Shoppe in New Castle, Pa., I've heard just about every justification there is for buying a train. My favorite is, "It's better for me to buy trains than to be gambling or spending money at some bar." I guess I can go along with that.

The justification that trains are good investments doesn't seem to work now, but it's still more fun to buy trains than to sock away money in that now-deflated IRA.

The best reason for buying trains is, "These trains are for my grandchildren, but I'm keeping them at home so the kids have something to play with when they visit." Wives usually accept this reason because nothing is too good for their grandchildren.

Many spouses don't understand the passion that drives collectors. Experience has taught me that this passion isn't based on a desire to deceive wives or make shrewd investments.

No, we love vintage trains because they rekindle the feelings of better times. We become boys again, innocent and free of any troubles.

We remember a time when we lived in a fantasy world, playing cowboys and Indians, pretending we were John Wayne, and thinking electric trains were the greatest gifts anyone could give us. Toy trains are the mental aspirin that helps us deal with today's complexities.

The smartest wives recognize our feelings and see that "little boy" when he is in a train shop or working on his layout. They know that money spent on toy trains is a good investment because it always pays dividends of happiness in the coming days and years.

Keep searchin'

2010

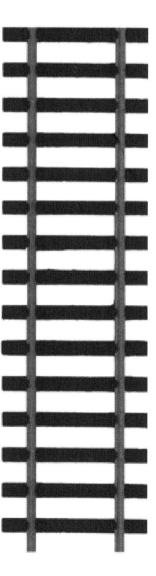

Where Have all the Lionels Gone?

Once upon a time at the turn of the 20th century, there was a man named Joshua. He produced toy trains for little boys,

Over the years, Joshua made trains in many shapes and sizes. Big Standard gauge *Blue Comets*, beautiful O gauge *Hiawathas*, and the most famous of them all, the Santa Fe *Super Chief* streamlined train in all its splendor.

These wonderful electric trains became the favorite toys of nearly every boy for more then 50 years, and every one of those trains was called "Lionel."

Every little boy wanted toys that resembled the mighty trains that moved the country. In those days, railroads were part of the landscape and trains provided a massive demonstration of force and speed. America was in love with trains and America's little boys were in love with toy trains.

However, in the sixth decade of the 20th century, the little boys no longer played with their Lionels. Race cars, airplanes, and spaceships won their hearts.

While the boys (no longer so little) focused on other toys and hobbies, most of the Lionels were put to rest in attics, cellars, and garages—the graveyards of childhood dreams. Some were given away, and many were thrown away.

The Lionels that weren't destroyed were ignored. For 20 years, these relics lay buried. Meanwhile, those boys grew into men. They finished schooling, took jobs, and started families of their own.

Then the day came when they wanted to relive the time that the Lionels brought them happiness. Those men realized they had lost something of value. They missed the Lionels that had rumbled over the hardwood floors of mansions and around Christmas trees in smaller homes.

The desire to find the old electric trains inflamed these men. Like an army, they fanned out across the country to search for the long-buried Lionels. They established organizations to share information and advance their search.

Newly published books and catalogs told the men which of the old relics were the most desired. Once enlightened, they placed ads in newspapers to let the world know of the army's mission. Hot, dusty attics were searched. Cold, moldy cellars were swept. The contents of garages were hauled into the sunlight and scrutinized.

"Soldiers" in this army paid high bounties for many of the relics that were preserved in their original condition. Old drugstores, old hardware stores, and other places where the relics had been sold were searched for forgotten signs, boxes, and wrappings. The soldiers sought to preserve every piece of Lionel history they could uncover.

A competition to see who had the most Lionels began. The army held meetings throughout the land to display, trade, or sell the spoils of the hunt, but only after keeping the best for themselves.

Thousands of soldiers attended these meetings to see and buy the meticulously cleaned and displayed relics. They even established a system by which to grade and rate the pieces. Many of the Lionels found in poor condition were restored to their original form.

A fraternity developed among the soldiers. To them, each train meet represented all the Christmases of years gone by. These meets were happy occasions.

More years passed. Soldiers insisted on buying and then keeping the best trains. There were no more Lionels buried in attics, forgotten in cellars, or left in damp garages. The army declared victory!

The soldiers returned home and built shrines to display their relics. They created beautiful layouts to honor the original intent of the toys. The meets were now filled with new replicas of the original Lionels. No longer would the bounties of the great hunt fill the halls. The old Lionels were gone again.

But time never stops, and the soldiers aged. Now they wonder what will happen when they're gone. Will their children's children understand the true worth of these treasures, or will the Lionels gather dust again and return to attics and cellars to await the arrival of a new army?

Where have all the Lionels gone? Gone to graveyards everywhere! When will they ever learn? When will they ever learn?

Keep Searchin'

CREATIVE ACCOUNTING
Your Trains are Really Worth More than You Imagine

A hobbyist told me that, to the best of his knowledge, he had lost more than $40,000 in the value of his postwar and modern-era trains over the past 10 years. His collection has gone down at least 40 percent during that time. He determined his loss by comparing what the latest price guides indicated his trains were worth against what they might have brought if he had sold them in the 1990s when their value was higher.

I tried to be sympathetic but then asked a few questions that all of us need to ask ourselves. I wondered why, in the 1980s and '90s, he had bought these Lionel trains in the first place. Did he buy them for the enjoyment of owning and operating? Or did he buy them as an investment, a way to make money, just like he might buy real estate, stocks and bonds, or gold?

The usual answer to these questions is: "All of the above." Of course, this fellow insisted he bought his trains to have fun. It's just that he also wanted them to increase in value. But wanting everything could be his—and our—problem.

During the 1980s and midway into the '90s, when this guy and other collectors spent a lot on trains, the values of those vintage and contemporary item were rising faster than the inflation rate. Folks thought this trend would last forever. Well, it didn't. The law of supply and demand took care of that.

People who visit my Underground Railroad Shoppe have told me they bought many of their toy trains in the 1980s and '90s so they could sell them 20 years later to augment their retirement income. Guess what? "20 years later" has arrived!

Looking back, many collectors bought their trains in the heat of the moment. With their friends, they competed to see who could amass the most and best trains. They justified much of this wild spending by telling themselves (and maybe their spouses) that buying trains was like "putting money in the bank."

Then money ran out and storage space dwindled. Collectors turned into dealers, as they sold their collections.

In my opinion, trains were never meant to be investments. The hobby is about having fun. Owning trains is a big part of the hobby, even if you decide not to run them or take them out of the box.

This hobby is also about making new friends—often from different walks of life and backgrounds. No matter how different we may be, what we have in common is a love of trains that very often dates from our childhood.

Fun and friends and good times—isn't that what taking up any hobby is all about? If you leave this hobby and get rid of your trains, anything you get out of them monetarily is simply a bonus. You've already been repaid many times.

I compare the train hobby with other hobbies and recreational expenses. The enjoyment is the net product; there usually is no money returned when the recreational activity is over. At least for now, there is a return on toy trains.

My wife and I took a trip to Italy. Our 15-day tour cost about $9,000 for the airfare and other travel expenses, accommodations, food, and souvenirs. We loved the trip, and came home with fantastic memories and enough photos to fill a dozen books, but none of the $9,000—which is what we expected.

If we look at money spent on trains in the same way – as bringing new experiences, wonderful memories, and lasting friends, we won't be disappointed.

Getting back to the guy who "lost" $40,000 on his collection. I asked what his trains are worth today. He said they're worth a little more than what he paid for them. So where, I ask, is that $40,000 loss? That's what I call "creative accounting."

Go figure!

They're Just Like Bricks
Toy Trains Can Go from Treasure to Cargo

Most of the train dealers I know started out as train collectors. I'm not talking about the owners of traditional hobby shops, who sell toy trains as part of their complete line of hobby merchandise (trains, plastic model kits, remote-controlled cars and helicopters, and more). I'm thinking about guys who buy and sell vintage trains at shows, over the Internet, or even in retail stores that specialize in trains.

Many of today's train dealers started selling trains in the late 1970s and early '80s. They actually began as collectors of trains, but ended up as dealers because they wanted to supplement their collecting dollars and dispose of items that for various reasons they decided they didn't want or need for their collection.

I started going to shows in the early '80s. Initially, I was a rabid collector. I attended every train meet possible and advertised in local newspapers. I also went to any little hobby shop I could find to add vintage models to my collection.

In response to my ads, I seemed to get phone calls every day from people eager to get rid of the old trains being stored in their garages, attics, and basements. After buying what they had and deciding what to keep, I took the rest, cleaned and repaired them, and sold them at meets almost every week.

It wasn't long before I met other guys doing the same thing, and we soon formed a fraternity that traveled to train shows all over the country.

We good-naturedly competed with each other to see who got the best buys of the week. It was all a lot of fun, and the fruits of the labor made everything worthwhile.

I always felt a slight resentment toward dealers who were not train collectors. I thought that those guys were not in the hobby for the love of toy trains but for the love of money. To me, they were members, not of the TCA (Train Collectors Association), but the MCA (Money Collectors Association).

I admit that my resentment was not justified. We all have a right to do what we want with our money. When I heard a few dealers boasting about how they didn't have a single train in their own homes, I felt sorry for them. They were missing out on the "high" that comes when you find an item you've been searching for in a dusty attic.

Back then, every train show started the same way. Before the public walked in, dealers were buying from other dealers to feed their train fevers. Guys would pay top dollar for items in pristine condition because they knew they would sell enough at the show to make up for their crazy spending spree.

I noticed that over the past decade many dealers lost the desire to collect. They became more intent on selling trains. They were no longer searching for that prize piece to add to their collection. The fire was gone.

A few dealers became successful businessmen who view toy trains less as treasure and more as cargo. One of the top dealers in America was once an avid collector of Lionel Standard gauge and other prewar trains. I wonder if he can still get excited over a *Blue Comet* outfit, like new, in the original box. I bet not.

Once I asked a dealer whom I used to sell trains to if he still searched for sets and models for his collection. He replied, "No, I don't collect them anymore and have sold most of my collection. I keep buying and selling trains, but they don't seem the same to me.

"They're just like bricks."

He's not alone. Other dealers who once collected say the same thing. What a shame!

I'm glad that I still have the fever. No matter how many trains I own, I can guarantee they'll always be treasures.

Keep searchin'!

Cottage Industries
The Little Guys Who Rock the Train World

Bob Leonowicz of R & L Lines recently asked me to try the new track-scrubbing car that his business produces and markets. I took the car over to my store (the Underground Railroad Shoppe in New Castle, Pa.) and set it loose on the O gauge layout there. The cleaner did a fantastic job on a railroad that has many hard-to-clean sections of track on 16 separate lines with seven tunnels.

Watching Bob's track cleaner caused me to think of all the new products that have been introduced to the toy train hobby since its resurgence in the 1970s. Specifically, I recalled how toy train enthusiasts developed so many of these products using knowledge and talent related to their everyday professions.

Most of these items are geared toward improving the appearance and operation of layouts. The track-cleaning car is a typical product that was developed by people using their work experience and relating it to the hobby.

Toy train hobbyists deserve credit for many other items that have changed the way we design, build, and run our O or S gauge layouts. Animated scenes, neon signs, die-cast metal figures, structure kits, trees, mountains, and trackside items are just a few of the innovative products that have hit our market.

These cottage businesses are not limited to the construction and operation of layouts. Train parts represent another area that has sparked the development of new small businesses. When collectors needed parts to repair and restore prewar and postwar trains, they manufactured and sold those parts. In doing that, they formed a large network of parts dealers. Screws, rivets, body parts, and electronic components are just a few cottage industries that are flourishing.

Collectors with knowledge of chemistry developed better smoke fluids. For example, Bob Board created Super Smoke, which smelled like that old American Flyer cedar scent. Who can forget that smell? Other people have followed suit, and a myriad of scents is available in toy train smoke fluid.

I started a small business after noticing the need for water-type decals that could be used to restore postwar Lionel trains. A friend of mine made the decals, which have found customers among hobbyists fixing up old rolling stock as well as with professional restoration experts, who specialize in painting and decorating damaged vintage locomotives and cars.

Another area that has attracted newcomers is toy train art. The best-known artist is Angela Trotta Thomas, who uses her abilities to create nostalgic train paintings, Christmas cards, and more. Angela's husband, Bob Thomas, introduced her to toy trains. They create great scenes, which Angela paints on canvas.

The electronic age has led collectors with computer knowledge to develop businesses that assist hobbyists with inventory and layout track designs.

Most of the folks launching cottage industries do this as a side business. The money they make augments their train budget. Some of them have turned their sideline into a lucrative business. They have found ways to use their talent to do something they like in a hobby they love while being their own boss.

Cottage industries are important to the well-being and growth of the toy train hobby. They are the cherry on top of the sundae that makes up the industry dominated by Atlas O, Bachmann Industries, Lionel, MTH, and other manufacturers, not to mention distributors, hobbyshop owners, and more.

It's amazing to stand back and look at what this hobby has turned into. And to think that it all started with kids running toy trains at the holidays.

Keep searchin'

Hi-Yo, Silver, Away!
A New Lionel Set Brings Back Wonderful Memories

I'll bet that as soon as you read the title of my column, you knew I was thinking about the Lone Ranger. That fictional character and his "faithful Indian companion, Tonto" starred, first on radio (1933-55) and then on television (1949-57).

Knowing that many baby boomers loved the Lone Ranger and Tonto almost as much as their electric toy trains probably led Lionel LLC to bring out the no. 30116 Lone Ranger Wild West Set with TrainSounds in 2009.

That O gauge three-car train features an updated version of the postwar General old-time steam locomotive and tender, plus an operating Lone Ranger and outlaw car, an old-style truss rod gondola with covered box loads, and a 19th-century baggage car with Wild West sounds.

After my store received a few of the Lone Ranger Wild West Sets, I couldn't wait to operate one. I was pleasantly surprised when I installed the battery in the baggage car. A flick of the switch and the familiar sounds of the old *Lone Ranger* TV program played.

Yes, it was the original adaptation of the *William Tell Overture* that was heard at the beginning of each TV show and during the final airing of the credits. And Lionel didn't give us a shortened version either. I heard the opening music, complete with gunshots and the famous "Hi-yo, Silver."

The Lone Ranger Wild West Set is a terrific train that revives a load of memories. The set even has a neat pair of Lone Ranger and Tonto scale figures, along with their horses, Silver and Scout. I'll bet that those ancillary items will become collectable, once original ones are lost.

The 4-4-0 locomotive is equipped with TrainSounds. However, I wish Lionel had invested in a new sound chip that played appropriate Western sounds, rather than the same tired TrainSounds chip that's been around for some time.

I displayed this set and demonstrated the sound car to everybody. I was amazed to discover how many people under 40 weren't familiar with the Lone Ranger. Children had no clue about the masked rider and his faithful friend.

I feel sad to realize how much these youngsters have missed. I don't know anyone in his 50s or 60s who didn't respect the Lone Ranger as played on TV by Clayton Moore. He's up there with Superman in my book. The black-and-white programs brought me hours of wholesome enjoyment as a boy.

When I demonstrate the baggage car for guys my age, I see a familiar smile on their face and gleam in their eyes. Funny thing – I notice the same traits at train shows. They explain why we love and collect toy trains.

The Lone Ranger Wild West Set suggests that Lionel is focusing on the demographic group that includes folks over the age of 50. That may also explain why, during this past holiday season, Lionel advertised on the *Don Imus In The Morning Show*, a TV show aimed at older people with money. Everyone knows that baby boomers still have purchasing power!

It's nice to see grandparents introducing trains to their grandkids. As a result, it didn't take long for a few of my younger shoppers to catch on to the fun created by the Lone Ranger Wild West Set. Kids like the train and figures. Grandmas and grandpas quickly put the Lone Ranger set on their gift list.

I added one of these sets to my own collection, but didn't take everything home. I left the sound-equipped baggage car on the counter of my store. Now I just flick the switch and return to a Saturday morning in the 1950s with that hearty "Hi-yo, Silver, away!"

Keep searchin'!

"She Loves You... Yeah, Yeah, Yeah!"
Toy Trains and Oldies Songs Have a Lot in Common

My wife and I recently attended a TRIBUTE 64 concert at the Stambaugh Auditorium in Youngstown, Ohio. TRIBUTE 64 is the number-one Beatles tribute band in the world. The talented musicians in the group look and sound exactly as I remember the Beatles more than 40 years ago.

While waiting for the show to start, I watched the crowd file into the auditorium. The gray hair on many attendees reminded me of the audience that I'd seen on the Lawrence Welk television show that my grandparents watched when I was a teen in the 1960s.

Then I started paying more attention to the folks joining me at the show and realized that a number of them were the age of my grandchildren. There were kids and teenagers, along with people in their 20s and 30s. Of course! The music of the Beatles appeals to everyone and always will.

Returning to the show my wife and I saw, I can guarantee you that everyone there, regardless of age, had a great time. The two-hour performance was quite thrilling even without all the screaming girls that usually accompanied a "real" Beatles performance in person or on television in the 1960s.

Since I am immersed in the toy train hobby, you won't be surprised that what I saw and heard at the concert in Youngstown got me thinking about what's going on with today's O and S gauge collectors and operators.

The face of train meets has changed over the past 30 years. More gray hair, but that's just the first impression; think more deeply and you'll realize that there's as much fun as ever.

There is still a lot of interest in the toy train hobby. I'm seeing recently retired guys starting to collect and operate trains. Vintage and new sets and models are great retirement fillers. I also see many youngsters getting into the hobby, thanks to their grandparents and Thomas the Tank Engine.

Building a layout is a longtime dream of many people. Now, with leisure time available, the dream can become a reality. More of my customers choose to share their dreams and make them real with their grandkids.

What else tells me that toy trains, like the Beatles, are standing the test of time? Let's keep in mind the huge success of Lionel's series of reissued outfits from the postwar era: Postwar Celebration and Conventional Classics. Because of these superb reissues, guys can buy the trains they wanted when they were young.

We might have to make the aisles at toy train shows a little wider to accommodate the ever-increasing number of motorized chairs, but that's an improvement for everyone.

My good friend Father Michael Ruthenburg, a retired priest at the home of the Little Sisters of the Poor in Chicago, constructed an O gauge train village at that facility. He reports that it is very popular with the residents, who line up to sit and watch the display run daily during the holiday season. This devout priest and toy train hobbyist has a great time sharing his interest with all the folks at his home.

People will always enjoy the tranquility that a layout gives and all the great memories that are brought to life. All of this goes on while listening to the background music, which typically includes songs by the Beatles. Together, they represent the sound track of our lives, whether we're senior citizens, baby boomers or members of Generation X.

Keep searchin'!

DETAIL TO RETAIL
Good Advice When You're Selling Toy Trains

In my early teens, one of my favorite places to hang out was a used car lot in my neighborhood, located on a street with eight other used car lots. That was where people shopped in my town in the 1950s when they wanted a used car.

I washed cars and ran endless errands for the salesmen. The pay was minimal, but you can be sure that I would have done it for nothing.

The guys there let me drive around the lot; sometimes I'd make short runs for them even though I was too young to get my driver's license in Pennsylvania.

Watching the salesmen practice their craft was an education for me. They knew how to treat people and sell cars. The salesmen always dressed well and worked hard during the week, then enjoyed a great card game every Friday night.

What made this business successful, besides the hard-working sales staff, was its ability to take cars that had been traded in or bought at auction and make them look brand new inside and out, while also making sure the cars ran well.

Another memory was hearing the salesmen brag about the people who returned to buy cars from them. Each person was referred to as "my customer." Return business is the mark of a good salesperson.

Why am I sharing these memories with you? Because I've discovered that the toy train hobby has a lot in common with the car business.

Much of it comes down to buying and selling new and used models and a vendor's approach to offering items.

I remember well hearing the salesmen at the used car lot say, "You have to detail to retail." By that phrase, they meant that good esthetics trigger any buying impulse.

"Detail to retail" came back to me years later when I started to buy and sell postwar and prewar trains. I make sure to clean each piece and check that it operates well before trying to sell it. Lionel ZW transformers exemplify my approach and illustrate why my ZWs sell for more than those offered by other vendors. If I don't have an original box, I supply a new reproduction box as well as a copy of instructions with each ZW.

I've learned many cleaning techniques over the years. Light dishwashing soap, a soft toothbrush, and warm water are my "tools" when starting to clean each item. My goal is to have each train looking like it has its original sheen and working like a fine clock. That's the way Lionel and Gilbert sold them long ago.

I often hear other vendors boast that they never "fix anything up" and just display their goods as they bought them. That's okay if you price vintage models as fair- or poor-graded trains. Instead, I find some vendors still pricing their used trains as though they were excellent or like-new. No surprise they end up lugging the same stuff from show to show because buyers aren't tempted to take a risk.

Another pet peeve of mine is dealers who don't put prices on their trains. I usually pass by any item that isn't priced. Anyone can miss pricing an item during setup, but some dealers deliberately leave off prices. They think they're being smart, but that's just poor business in my book.

Most of the toy trains that I've sold over the past 30 years have been used (I call them "pre-owned"). Every day, I feel like I'm reaching back to and using the knowledge that I received while working at the used car lot.

Above all, learn to treat people well and always "detail to retail."

Keep searchin'!

THE STUFF OF OUR DREAMS
We Have Become a Nation of Collectors

Admit it—you have a lot of "stuff" in your home. And the toy trains —O, S, Standard, and other gauges—are just the beginning. We've become a nation of collectors, and there's absolutely not a thing that doesn't have people interested in owning it.

Let me tell you about my own obsessions. I was sitting in my bar room, looking at all the stuff I've placed in this special part of my house. It was filled with all the things that I like, most of them items related to days gone by.

In one corner I have a Seeburg jukebox (much like the one seen on the old TV series *Happy Days*) that I've loaded with 45-rpm records from the 1950s and '60s. Nearby there's a Vendo Coke machine (it still works), and a beautifully restored Texaco gas pump with a matching red Echo air pump (the kind with a window and a handle on the side) that you frequently saw at filling stations during the postwar era.

That isn't all. I collect vintage neon signs, Coca-Cola memorabilia, and all sorts of trinkets from old soda shops from the time that I grew up. The walls of my favorite room are hung with framed movie posters from the 1950s, the sole exception being one showing Marlon Brando's character in *The Godfather*, from 1972.

Guess what? You won't find any vintage electric trains or tin toys in this room. But that doesn't mean I don't collect those, too. They, like my old baseball cards, are in another room reserved especially for them. In addition, that's where I keep and display my vintage pedal cars, die-cast vehicles, lead soldiers, and comic books. I like them all, but will confess that trains are my top collectible.

Each of these different kinds of "stuff" has a group of people chasing after them. We call these people collectors—they love to hunt and gather these items.

Organizations emerge for the sole purpose of sharing the bounties of these collectors. Many businesses develop for buying, selling, and trading these gems. Like toy train collectors, these folks are asking the questions about the longevity of their respective hobbies. That still hasn't diminished the collecting fever.

The funny thing about collecting is that, speaking in all honesty, we don't need any of this stuff. We collect for the pure enjoyment of finding these treasured items and owning them. Sometimes we use our stuff, but mostly the feeling of possessing it gives us enough satisfaction. In fact, we get the greatest satisfaction out of finding something after spending a long time searching for it.

All of the items I collect, not to mention hotrods from the 1950s and muscle cars from the '60s (about the only stuff I don't collect), have become icons of the popular culture of postwar America. That's why they'll be collected forever. I think it is human nature to hunt and collect stuff we think is neat.

Electric trains rank near the top of modern collectibles. And believe me, we're at the beginning of that collecting era. Toy trains have been recognized, categorized, and organized into a great collector item. Plus, they *can* be used.

There's a saying that a boat owner's two best days are the day he buys it and the day he sells it. I don't think that applies to any collector hobby. Instead, there is an emotional tie to the items we collect, and it's a sad day when they are sold. It's my feeling that generations to come will collect and cherish these items and stuff associated with the future. Let me know what you collect and why.

Keep searchin'

DIFFERENT STROKES
Is the Toy Train Hobby Becoming Polarized?

I have a bin in the front of my store (The Underground Railroad Shoppe in New Castle, Pa.) that I keep filled with bargains. Folks discover rolling stock, locomotives, parts, and other train-related items priced below $20.

The bargain bin tends to be a popular stop for customers, especially since I'm constantly restocking it with more goodies. It's the first and last thing people, regardless of age or experience with trains, like to dig through when they come in.

Funny how the adults and kids who like to forage in the bargain bin seem to have less in common in their approach to the hobby. I believe we're seeing more divisions, even polarizing differences among toy train enthusiasts.

On one hand, more people are content with just operating their O and S gauge trains, often items they've fixed or restored to run on their layouts.

Hobbyists in this first group may take an old metal tank car, for example, strip off the original paint and graphics, and repaint it. Then they apply new decals and have a new model to run, a car that blends the past with the present.

The guys into restoration say the work is enjoyable, particularly during those long winter nights. They also cannibalize the cheap items I sell for parts, as they plan future projects at a time when the economy has affected them.

In addition, an increasing number of collectors are fixing up junkers and selling them at shows or online. They're careful to note their handiwork is just that—a restoration and not a pristine original deserving of a very high price.

I enjoy finding locomotives and cars with the potential to be cleaned and repaired so they can become collector's pieces. Bringing a train back to life after its original sheen has dulled and its beauty has faded is enjoyable.

Many times I've uncovered vintage Lionel or American Flyer trains in a dusty attic that were in like-new condition when someone put them there but that have since lost their glory. Time and inadequate storage methods have hurt the condition of these trains and their boxes. It takes a lot of patience and experience to restore their luster and give them a like-new appearance.

At the other spectrum of the train hobby I put the ever-increasing number of operators who like to buy new and expensive trains only. They spend money like they're mad at it!

Fans of the latest O and S gauge equipment insist on getting all the new sounds and features. Their layouts are large and consist of many switches and different railroad lines. They also favor command control. Lionel and MTH are constantly upgrading their systems to accommodate them.

I like to watch toy train enthusiasts in this second camp operate these new trains on their big layouts with all the fancy maneuvers they can do. Their favorite locomotives tend to be scale steamers retailing for $1,000 and up. Some guys own more then 20 of these top-of-the-line steamers.

I don't know what sort of layout can accommodate so many large engines, but these customers claim they run them all. As for me, I prefer older locomotives, the kind I had as a youngster in 1950 with only a whistle and smoke.

There you have it: Two groups in the hobby that seem to be growing—and growing further apart. Perhaps there are more toy train enthusiasts in the middle than I recognize, but I think it's important to point out this divide.

So am I wrong about all of this? Am I exaggerating current divisions in the hobby? Or has it always been this way? Please let me know, because I always like reading *your* points of view.

Keep searchin'!

2011

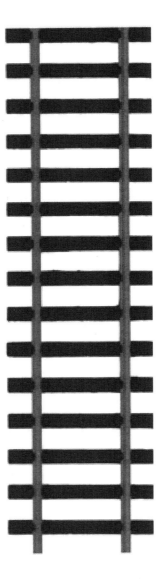

WARM FEELINGS
Winter is Not So Bad When You Have Toy Trains

Here we are in another winter season. I live in western Pennsylvania, and let me tell you that it can get very cold here in the Keystone State.

I enjoy the changes each season brings, but I really feel that winter is the best season for playing with toy trains. This is the time of year when the days become shorter and the nights last so much longer. Temperatures become a lot colder, and those of us living in the Northeast and Midwest can get snow in very large amounts.

All of these factors cause folks to retreat to their basements, where their train rooms are usually located. I don't think there's anything much better than sitting in your train room on a snowy winter night and getting lost in your O or S gauge train layout. A cup of coffee or hot chocolate is a good start for a most pleasurable evening spent "working" on trains or adding scenery and details to your layout.

Of course, the center point of any winter is the holiday season that arrives right after Thanksgiving and lasts through the coming of the new year. Every since I can remember, the annual holiday season has consistently been enhanced in every way by the train hobby. People just automatically tie toy trains of all sizes and Christmas or Chanukah together.

These electric jewels stoke wonderful memories of holidays past as they fly along the trackside scenes we've created in our miniature fantasy villages. Many winter scenes can also be found on layouts, especially those constructed beneath Christmas trees.

To be honest with you, I've always felt a bit sorry for those folks who don't have train rooms to take refuge in to avoid the frigid long northern winter nights. The warm feelings we get are kind of neat, when the early sunsets give us plenty of time, since outdoor chores are put to a stop once winter comes.

I enjoy reading and researching the train material that I gather during the year, like rereading old issues of *Classic Toy Trains*, as well as other train-related articles. There are volumes of printed items that are enjoyable to catch up on while I'm relaxing in my train room.

This is also the time of year when I look back and reflect on what I see going on the toy train hobby. Besides being a dedicated hobbyist, I am the owner of a toy train store, so I get a good idea of what is happening. For me, 2010 has been an interesting year in the train hobby.

The economy remains in a slump, but I still see a lot of new and vintage trains being bought and sold.

Lionel announced that it's not going to produce the K-Line products any longer. I hope someone else resumes K-Line production. That firm had a lot of nice trains and accessories.

Baby boomers born in 1945, right after World War II, became 65 years old. Many baby boomers are already in the hobby, but I'm seeing more newly retired guys getting into the hobby. They're looking for a great leisure-time activity, and trains are a good fit for many newly retired folks.

I'm seeing that now in my store and I believe this trend will continue at least for the next 10 years.

We will have to see what the new year brings, although I know one thing that it does for me—it gets me out of Pennsylvania! I know I said I love the winter months, but I usually spend three or four weeks of

February in Florida to thaw out and get ready for spring and the April train show in York, Pa! Then the cycle begins again.

Happy holidays from the Palumbo family and the Underground Railroad Shoppe and keep searchin'

Rolling Stock Overload
Are There too Many Reefers on the Market?

Like many of you, I remember the early 1980s, when many pieces of O gauge rolling stock were considered collectable. Lionel introduced new boxcars in various road names, and a wide assortment of billboard refrigerator cars hit the market.

You had to buy a copy of the annual pocket price guide to Lionel trains put out by Greenberg Publishing Co. (now by Kalmbach Publishing Co.) to keep up with the values of these freight cars. Most of them were cheaply built with plastic trucks, but all were colorful.

To give you an idea of how prices were out of control, the caramel version of the Lionel no. 9853 Cracker Jack refrigerator car was selling for $40 to $80. In retrospect, it was crazy how cars rose in value.

We toy train enthusiasts were desperate for new items and could not help getting caught up in the collecting frenzy. We worried that the spigot would be closed again and trains would become extinct.

I remembered the time in the 1960s when American Flyer left us and Lionel seemed to lose direction. We had felt like train orphans. This time we bought every model Lionel was producing, so we were well supplied and wouldn't have to face a future without trains.

Today, of course, you and I know that is not what happened. Instead, Lionel kept putting out trains as fast as it could. In the 1990s and after, new companies—Atlas O, K-Line, MTH, Weaver, and others—jumped into the game. The quality of O gauge trains kept improving, and the quantity of new cars being made was absolutely staggering.

Tons of rolling stock hit the market. Every year beautiful boxcars, reefers, tank cars, and cabooses filled the new catalogs from all the different companies. On top of that, Lionel and its peers would make "collector" cars for everybody. Train clubs, manufacturers, and everyone else seemed to have "limited-production" commemorative cars made. These models are all over the place now.

Enough all ready! How much rolling stock can we force into the market?

Rather than cranking out more basic freight cars, toy train firms should use their engineering expertise to develop new models of exceptional types of cars and be sure they don't cost an arm and a leg! Let them bring out operating cars for those folks who still play with trains.

Put simply, when it comes to rolling stock, manufacturers need to "think outside the boxcar" to interest those of us in the hobby.

Lionel made an excellent start on this with the different add-on cars it has been developing to broaden the appeal of its *Polar Express* train set.

Firms need to create a broader range of new action cars. The Lionel no. 29800 command-control crane car introduced in 2004 and the similar models that followed were terrific, but they've been priced too high for average train guys.

Companies have made good operating cars—but not enough of them. Lionel should continue to make a lot of the old K-Line operating items, including the dump cars and the milk car.

In addition to all the new rolling stock, we have watched as many collections have been pushed onto the market. I feel sorry for people who want to sell a collection with hundreds of boxcars and reefers, along with some engines. They're shocked to learn that the value of most of the cars bought in the 1970s and '80s has fallen over the decades.

In short, if Lionel, MTH, and others never make another reefer or boxcar for the O gauge market, well, there are enough on the planet to go around!

The Cracker Jack refrigerator car mentioned earlier proves my point. Examples, whether white or caramel, sell for around $15 to $20 these days.

Keep searchin'

ON THE OTHER HAND...
Not Every Train from the Postwar Era was a Classic

I read with great enjoyment my buddy Roger Carp's latest book, *101 Classic Toy Trains: Best of the Postwar Years* (item no. 64100, available for $24.95 from www.KalmbachBooks.com). I recommend this book for anyone who likes postwar toy trains and accessories and their history.

Many of my all-time favorites are included in Roger's list of the finest trains made between 1945 and 1969. Of course, I have to disagree with him, too.

I doubt if I would have given Lionel's operating milk car as high a ranking as Roger did. In fact, that postwar favorite would not have made my top 101 list. But then that's why Baskin-Robbins has 31 flavors of ice cream.

The toy train item I find is remembered most fondly by those of us who grew up in the postwar era is the smoke pill Lionel developed. Everyone seems to recall putting little pills into the smokestacks of steam engines and watching them smoke. Smoke pills really impressed those children!

Being the kind of guy I am, I can't resist taking the opposite approach from Roger and mentioning some of my all-time losers among postwar trains.

Let's start with the first rotary beacons put out by Lionel, American Flyer, Colber, and Marx. All of them were designed with a red-and-green beacon sitting on top of a light bulb with a dimple molded into the glass bulb. The beacon top had a needle post that sat in the dimple; heat passing through metal deflectors on the top of the beacon would cause it to turn.

Too bad motion occurred only when the temperature was just right in the room and there were no air drafts. Most of the time, the beacon would just sit there. Then usually any slight bump or draft from the furnace would make the beacon slip onto the bulb and burn a hole in one of the plastic lenses. Most of the used beacons that I buy today have a hole or two in the beacon top.

Thankfully, Lionel eventually replaced its poorly performing no. 394 with the no. 494 rotary beacon. An electric vibrating coil handled the movement of the beacon. I have had one of these accessories on my layout for many years.

The second losers are the Lionel and Gilbert operating stockyards. They get high points for looks. However, the American Flyer no. K771 stockyard has much more detail than the Lionel no. 3656.

These two accessories have a great presence on the layout, but are big losers when it comes to operation. They should have been called the "Dancing Cows." When the cows are assembled in the stockyard and a switch is thrown to start the animation, they look like they're dancing the Macarena!

As most postwar enthusiasts know, the cows seldom make it up the ramp into the waiting stockcar. Instead, they fall down like they had too much to drink. The cows that do make it into the car usually get stuck inside and never come out. The stockyards should have been made as non-operating accessories.

Finally, I would like to mention the air-chime whistle that Gilbert developed for its steam locomotives. When it worked (and that was chancy), it sounded like a buzzer or the static you hear coming through a cheap speaker.

Rather than end on a sour note, I want to add that my American Flyer layout included a whistling billboard whose sound was as good as the whistle Lionel installed on its locomotives. Better yet, Gilbert's whistle worked even while the train was going slow.

If you have anything you'd like to add to my list of "postwar losers," please let me know. When I have 101 of them, I'll write a book to compete with Roger's!

Keep searchin'!

MADE IN THE U.S.A.
Do You Really Care Where Your Trains are Made?

Not long ago, a woman walked into my store (the Underground Railroad Shoppe in New Castle, Pa.) with an interesting request. She was shopping for an O gauge train set for her husband, who was going to start a railroad for their grandchildren.

I started to point out the latest starter sets from Lionel and MTH. That's when the woman politely stopped my sales pitch and explained that her husband didn't want just any toy train.

He insisted anything she consider buying must have been made in America. She said that he was "like that" and would return anything not manufactured in the U.S.

The man's stipulation caught me by surprise. It didn't take long for me to realize that this ruled out any of the Lionel and MTH ready-to-run sets I would have recommended as a starting point with his railroad. What should I do now?

The answer quickly became obvious. I would have to ignore my new inventory and look over at the Lionel O gauge trains I had in stock from the postwar period (1945-69) and much of the modern era (1970 to the present).

I managed to put together a freight train led by a Lionel no. 675 steam locomotive and tender equipped with a smoke unit and a whistle. The woman wanted a "good smoker" for their grandkids and so was impressed with the durability and performance of this postwar engine that was in like-new condition.

Behind the locomotive, the woman and her husband preferred freight cars to passenger cars. It didn't take me long to scrounge up a nice selection of Lionel models made by General Mills Fundimensions in the 1970s and Lionel LLC from the 1980s and early '90s—all made in Mount Clemens, Mich.

I told the woman I didn't have any new American-made three-rail track, but could "hook her up" with used O gauge track and a no. 1033 90-watt transformer from Lionel. Even the lockon had been produced in the U.S.

This man and his wife aren't the only toy train enthusiasts concerned about where their locomotives, cars, and more are made. That's why Lionel is producing a set of Presidential boxcars made in the U.S.A., as shown in its 2010 catalog. I like this move and hope it's a sign of things to come.

Readers of *Classic Toy Trains* grew up knowing the words "Made in the U.S.A" indicated an item of quality. They—this includes yours truly— knew any product bearing this mark was superior to similar things made in other countries.

I'm sad to say this generalization no longer seems true—but how many people really care? In toy trains, new products made overseas have been beautiful. Much of the work is superior to what was done here in the 1970s and '80s.

However, I am familiar with some collectors who collect only those trains made in the U.S.A. I know that America can manufacture the same products that are now made overseas, if given the challenge. I don't know anything about the economics, but I would much rather be in a hobby that supports American-made products. Any company that does that would become number one in my book.

The man who insisted on American-made trains may not have been far off the mark. I know the hobby is not going to solve our economic problems, but the idea of increasing the number of models made here deserves consideration.

Electric trains are as American as baseball and apple pie. They serve as a reminder of days gone by, especially after World War II, when we played with all of those toy trains. Trains are a part of American history; it would be nice if the present-day replicas of those historic toys were manufactured in the U.S.A.

Keep searchin'!

It's Never the Same, But It's Still Okay
Toy Trains Come Close to Capturing Our Past

Have you tried to re-create an event from your life you remembered as great and found you just couldn't get the same results? There's always something missing from what you end up with, but even though it's never the same as you recall, you still feel like everything is usually okay.

That situation reminds me of the Bazooka bubble gum I used to put in a small dish next to my bed, when I was young. Mom never wanted me to chew gum in bed because she was afraid I would fall asleep and choke. So she put a dish on my bed stand and told me to deposit the gum there before getting into bed.

The moment I woke up I'd pop the gum in my mouth. Somehow, it never tasted as good the next day, but it was still okay.

The great memories that many readers of *Classic Toy Trains*, including me, have of the toy trains from their youth are something else that many have tried to re-create with varying degrees of success. Recently, I received an email from a friend that demonstrated the re-creation of nostalgic moments we all crave.

Attached to the message was a slideshow of pictures titled, "A very old city in the 1950s." This group of photos looked exactly like what I remembered of scenes from a small town 50 or 60 years ago. I felt good viewing this slideshow because it brought back the magic of those days.

Scenes were re-created using model homes, buildings, and vehicles, all in 1:24 scale. Each scene was masterfully detailed, with lighting and other effects suggesting rain and snow, daytime and night.

Another friend, Jeb Kriigel, does the same thing with railroad prints he creates with smaller models (1:48 scale). Still, his photographed scenes look authentic and are true art.

We try to re-create the O or S gauge layouts that we built during our childhood. I think the feeling I got when I was watching the slideshow is what we are all searching for. Although we know we will never bring back those days, the layouts we design and make can be worthwhile substitutes. That's why the research and construction turn out to be a lot of fun.

Collectors often try to accomplish the same goal. I've encountered many guys who are trying to find the same trains that they used to own, looking for the exact train set and accessories that were on their first layout. Some get intense in this search, even down to hunting for original smoke pills and grease kits. Original catalogs and related paper material are also included on their lists.

I have buddies who do the same thing with cars they drove when they were teenagers in the 1950s and '60s. It's not uncommon for a bunch of them to drive their vintage autos to a "car cruise" and sit around looking at the other vehicles. I may not get a kick out of that, but as a guy who has been to hundreds of train meets, I understand the thrill "motor heads" get from cruising.

What comes to mind when thinking about these people is nostalgia. That's a longing for something in the past, a time when you felt comfortable and safe from troubles. Nostalgia is made up of two Greek words that mean "returning home." That yearning drives many of us to spend money and energy chasing those great feelings we get when reminiscing about good times from long ago.

The toy train hobby allows us to search for those feelings. It's good, and it's innocent. More people should have a hobby that brings back great memories and lets them fill their leisure time in a good way. We are better people for it.

Keep searchin'!

Hot Peppers!
Trains Can Sizzle During the Summer Months

The summer months are always a lot of fun for my family and me. This is the time of year when I spend lots of time gardening.

I have a small "salad garden," as I call it, where I grow lettuce, tomatoes, onions, and garlic. I also have a few large pots in our yard so I can grow herbs.

Too bad my garden isn't big enough to provide our family with produce for another of my favorite summer pastimes: canning eggplant and hot peppers. I love these items when they're canned in oil flavored with spices. They make any sandwich fit for a king!

Another one of my favorite summer activities is going to local flea markets to purchase baskets of these vegetables, which will soon become a delicious meal once they are prepared and ready to be served. The flea markets also provide me a chance to search for hidden treasures to add to my toy train collection.

In all the years that I have been collecting vintage electric trains, I have discovered many great finds at flea markets near my home in western Pennsylvania. The regular dealers usually scavenge the best buys early, so I better arrive before the market opens if I want a good shot at finding a great collectible. I've seen guys holding flashlights while they look into boxes that are ready to be set up in the early mornings on flea market sale days.

New vendors, usually one-time sellers, are terrific sources if you hope to find good items. Many of these newcomers are cleaning out their attics and basements and just want to sell everything in a single trip to the market.

The regular vendors look for these folks during the early setup time. They gather like vultures and buy items as they're being unpacked by the new vendor. Most of those items will surely appear on their tables later that day.

Usually, toy trains can still be bought at a good price since most of the vendors are not "real" collectors anyway. I've also learned that it's smart to check on vendors who regularly sell trains.

However, because the one-time vendors usually offer the very best buys, the early bird gets the worm. That's why I love flea markets almost as much as my homegrown peppers! Nothing can beat walking around rows and rows of tables full of stuff on a nice summer day as you're looking for a postwar set box full of like-new Lionel, Marx, or American Flyer boxes that the vendor just unloaded from his truck to the table.

We all know finding items like these is a rare occasion now, but that doesn't keep us from hoping and searching. It's just like fishing. The line goes in, and the fisherman never knows when he or she is going to snag the "big one."

In addition, I like to search for other examples of postwar "non-train" memorabilia that I collect at these sales. My wife is going to have the mother of all flea markets when I "check out."

Yard sales are another summertime activity that can provide some nice train finds. I seldom go to these events, but I know some collectors who spend many Saturday mornings going to all the yard sales in the area.

You won't be surprised to learn that these guys usually bring most of the trains they buy into my shop for repairs. Every now and then they get a great item at a very good price. It's always the hunt that keeps the thrill in the hobby.

This is a great hobby. It provides a lot of fun in so many ways. As for me, toy trains have brought so much enjoyment to me during my years of retirement.

That being said, my second favorite thing in the summer is delicious, thinly sliced eggplant in garlic and oil on a piece of freshly baked bread and a nice jar of homemade hot peppers!

Keep searchin'

WALKING INTO THE 1950s
I Stepped into a Time Machine and Found Treasure

It's the recurring nightmare. You know the one. Your buddy calls out of the blue. His next-door neighbor has passed away, and the family is disposing of some vintage toy trains. A dealer is on the way, but if you want to have a look at the trains you can come over.

The nightmare part is you have been unemployed for the past six months and have only $100.

Here I was, living that nightmare, watching the fuel gauge on my truck moving toward empty and hoping to get another 60 miles out of what was left in the tank. Yet I was on a Lionel high.

What awaited me at journey's end? The only clue I had was the owner died at age 90 and had a reputation for buying the very best. The set was said to be in its original box and in good condition. That's all my buddy Bob could tell me over the phone. Visions of Lionel 400Es and 700Es filled my head.

I pulled into Bob's at the appointed time of 9 o'clock sharp. There was no sign of the Acme Antique truck in the neighbor's driveway so at least that part of the nightmare had not come true.

After the pleasantries, Bob and I walked over to the neighbors and let ourselves in. The house was in a little disarray as it was being prepared for sale. Nevertheless, I instantly felt at home. The place was decorated in the Colonial America style so common in the 1950s.

I walked into the kitchen and stopped in amazement. It was as if I had stepped into a time machine and been transported back to 1950. The maple kitchen cabinets were in perfect condition. The ancient Westinghouse refrigerator looked like it had just been delivered, and the delivery men had been careful not to scratch the linoleum floor. The thought that the next owner would certainly tear out all of this put a lump in my throat.

And then the door to heaven opened and we descended into the basement!

For those of you who did not grow up in the '50s, an explanation is required. Long ago, most basements were dark, damp places that housed the coal bin, furnace, and assorted plumbing.

Starting sometime in the 1930s, women's magazines began to run articles with titles like, "Convert Your Basement into a Rec-room."

After the war, young wives of the day would cut out these articles and badger their ex-GI husbands to turn their basement into a cocktail party paradise.

Bob and I found ourselves in a pristine example of a circa-1950 rec-room, complete with solid knotty-pine walls and built-in cabinets. I was in no hurry to see the trains. One look at this room told me the only remaining question was, would the F3 set (*of course* it would be F3s!) be in Santa Fe or New York Central colors.

It proved to be a New York Central F3 outfit, although the B unit was a bonus, along with a no. 624 switcher in a box complete with the Lionel wrapping paper. I wanted the set badly, but I couldn't bring myself to steal it for the $100 I had. So I told Bob its actual value, adding that the dealer should offer about 40 percent.

I was feeling gloomy, but then Bob pointed out a pile of track. Apparently at one time there had been an extensive layout in this 1950s haven of Middle America, made with GarGraves track. The track was in rough shape. I told Bob it was worthless to a dealer – and that's when I spotted them. At the bottom of the pile of track were Tremont switches. How did I know they were Tremonts? I had just read about them in the December 1953 issue of *Model Railroader*.

You see, I really needed a couple of frog-less switches for my layout, the kind of switches made about 60 years ago.

I thought I'd have to go back to 1953 to get them, but here I was in this time capsule of a room with the switches in my hands. Bob gave them to me free.

We lingered awhile, reluctant to leave. Then, as if we were in an episode of *The Twilight Zone*, we walked out of the front door and back into the year 2011.

Keep Searchin'

GOT TRAINS?
Conversations with Today's Hobbyists

I really enjoy meeting the folks who read *Classic Toy Trains* and express their interest in this column. I also want to acknowledge the emails, letters, and telephone calls I have received from you. I get a lot of good feedback and ideas for future columns, and your comments, even when you disagree with what I wrote, are all appreciated.

One place I get to hear what people think about this hobby is the semi-annual meet organized by the Eastern Division of the Train Collectors Association in York, Pa. Everybody who loves toy trains should plan to attend York at least once. You'll never see so many trains in one place or have such great opportunities to expand your knowledge of this great hobby.

At a recent York meet, I got a chance to talk to some CTT readers, who were eager to share their thoughts on the hobby of today and tomorrow.

Listen to what these guys had to say. Their views probably reflect many of your own ideas and will show you how deeply they feel about our hobby:

> SCOTT PALMER, age 37, an S gauge collector says, "The prices of new trains have to be controlled to get more interest in new trains."

GREGG AUSSEY, age 63 from High Point, N.C., is very passionate in his love for the hobby and feels the esthetics of trains is very important. "The looks of the trains" drives his collecting impulses.

ED SESSLEY, age 62 of Columbus, Ohio, gets a lot of satisfaction volunteering his time to build layouts for elementary students in area schools.

PHILLIP SPINATO, age 62 of Port Washington, N.Y., says, "We must get kids involved – they're the future of toy trains."

MIKE SALVATORE, age 54 of Wilmington, Del., prefers the old trains and said, "Electronics have to go."

JOE ROMANO, age 43 of Phoenixville, Pa., says he "Can't get enough of toy trains." He also added that Thomas the Tank Engine has helped the younger kids get interested.

FRANK TRAVISANO, age 65 of Middlesex, N.J., remembers trains since he was a little guy. His grandfather worked for Lionel at its factories in Newark and Irvington, N.J. Frank always had something new from Lionel at Christmas and would definitely like those days returned, "When trains were made in the U.S.A."

PETE MELONAS, 53, from Weirton, W. Va., has been collecting trains since the 1980s when you could sum up the state of the toy train hobby with "same thing/

different color." Now the best words are: "It's on the water" – meaning, something is on its way here from China. Still, Pete and his wife are always "searching."

And finally, I thought that **ED STERLING** of Winchester, Va., had an interesting comment: "All of the train manufactures should get together and advertise to build the hobby." I agree with Ed. The national dairy manufacturers did the same thing with their "Got milk?" campaign.

Atlas O, Bachmann, Lionel, MTH, Weaver, and related O gauge manufacturers should form a cooperative advertisement program. The media could be blitzed, especially during the holiday season, with ads promoting the hobby.

Ads should also be directed towards parents and grandparents who are looking towards retirement. Granddads and grandchildren can bond with a model train layout. Ads can be geared to kids, who realize the fun toy trains can be.

It takes a lot of money to promote the hobby, but a joint venture by manufacturers would get more bang for the buck.

I know this is not a new idea, but it's worth consideration by the people who make these decisions in toy train manufacturing. An intense ad campaign would be a fast transfusion of new blood in a hobby that could use it. "Got trains?"

Keep searchin'!

Meet Today's "Back-On-Track Train People"
Retirees are Discovering the Joys of Toy Trains

Did you know that more people are now reaching retirement age than at any other time in America's history? I've become aware of that because of something I see regularly at my store, the Underground Railroad Shoppe, in New Castle, Pa.

I'm noticing more and more guys who, after retiring, get involved in the hobby of toy trains. It's interesting to watch as these "new" enthusiasts start to collect and operate vintage and contemporary toy trains.

The scenario I hear about usually begins when a fellow who has recently retired discovers his boyhood train set when he is cleaning out the attic or cellar. This discovery renews the guy's interest in trains, and the journey begins. Often he has grandchildren who also get interested in the newly found hobby.

So what is the first thing this fellow does? He visits his local train store and enters the exciting world of trains. With that visit he learns that trains are still being produced and a lot has been done to promote and improve the hobby since he last played with his American Flyer or Lionel trains back in the 1950s.

Very soon, this fellow starts working on the layout of his dreams. Now our hobby is providing him with an excellent opportunity to start a project in his home that will entertain and challenge him as well as his grandchildren.

The train store becomes a regular stop for guys like him. It's a good place to see all the new train products, not to mention older trains and accessories. Further, traditional train stores provide an excellent repair and parts service.

I've seen tears in grown men's eyes when they see the old train they brought in for repair chugging around the track for the first time in years. They smell the smoke and ozone and hear a familiar whistle, and memories of holidays past are unlocked from deep in their minds.

Wives understand what is happening to the men they love and are pleased. No wonder some of my older customers are dropped off at the Underground Railroad Shoppe by the "missus" and left there while she does her shopping.

I enjoy the entertaining conversation that goes on among the train guys who hang out at the shop. They're always willing to share their ideas, and it's fun to see a "new" collector getting schooled by veteran hobbyists.

The talk can become spirited and loud—probably because many older train guys are "hearing challenged," myself included. I guess that goes with retirement scene. Once the talking begins and somebody starts to run a train with sounds, it gets intense, but is always in good fun and fellowship.

One by one the guys get picked up and returned to their own layout fantasy land. They'll tell you that a day at the Underground Railroad Shoppe or any other good train store is always interesting and enjoyable. Even better are those days when someone uncovers an item that has been on his wish list forever.

New ideas for a layout and tips on collecting, detailing, operating, and more can usually be found during a train shop visit. Lionel versus MTH, O gauge or S gauge, new trains verses old, conventional control or command: These are some of the subjects broached by the gang. Folks never run short of opinions, and everybody gets to have his say.

I look forward to visits with the "back-on-track train people." We have found a way to enjoy our retirement years, which is another reason that toy trains are such a great hobby.

Keep searchin'

2012

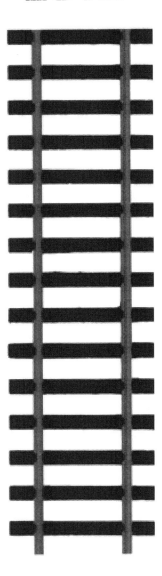

'TWAS THE WEEK AFTER CHRISTMAS
Bargains Hit the Stores after December 25th

When I was growing up in the 1950s, my favorite time of the year just might have been the week after Christmas. The days between Christmas and New Year's seemed like the ideal time for boys like me to find a lot of fun things to do.

A much-needed break from daily schoolwork was filled with days to enjoy our newly acquired Christmas gifts. The local movie house had special morning cartoon shows that were followed by a terrific cowboy double feature. During our Christmas break, managers of the local theaters would raffle off a bicycle to one lucky kid. I never won a bike, but I always looked forward to the drawing.

My buddies and I would finish the week by dragging the discarded Christmas trees in my neighborhood to the nearby baseball field. We built two huge forts for snowball fights.

Meanwhile, the stores that sold electric trains during the holiday season would sell the leftover stock at greatly reduced prices after Christmas. And back in the 1940s and '50s, many, many stores sold American Flyer, Lionel, and Marx trains.

Of course, the hobby shops carried trains throughout the year. But during the holiday season trains could be bought almost anywhere. Stores that sold tires and automotive parts, hardware and appliances, and groceries carried trains, as did drugstores and even filling stations.

Dealers ordered their trains in the spring, after the annual American Toy Fair in New York City. Sets and transformers, track and accessories, and more were shipped to the stores during the year.

Those stores sold trains at retail cost (twice the wholesale cost). They didn't have to pay for them until after the new year began, which was a good deal for the people who were selling them.

Then came the week after Christmas. That's when the stores dumped the entire unsold inventory at half price. My favorite thing was to go to the large department stores to see their holiday displays and the latest products from Lionel and Gilbert. There were incredible bargains for those of us lucky enough to have received a few dollars for Christmas or Chanukah.

My pals and I would spend hours visiting each store. After going to the stores, we tried to decide what to buy with all of our loot. Somehow, though, we never had enough money to get the best toy trains.

I could have bought a new Lionel Canadian Pacific F3 four-car passenger set, but who had $45? Instead I brought an American Flyer no. 694 green heavyweight observation for $3 to add to my collection.

When we were not outside riding our sleds, throwing snowballs, or going to morning movies, we were at each other's houses enjoying our new purchases for our train layouts. We worked on our layouts, building scenery and running trains.

On the Saturday between Christmas and New Year's, the local Y.M.C.A. had great O and S train races. Kids would bring their fastest locomotives and race them against each other. The races were exciting and fun. No, I never won!

Trains provided many good times for kids growing up in my generation.

The memories are tunneled deep in our minds and are nice to revisit. As for the Christmas tree forts, they provided a great activity during the winter. By March the trees were brown and dry. Then we would stack them up and have the traditional bonfire. Then we removed the ashes so that baseball season could start.

What a time! I'm really glad I was there...like so many of you!

Keep searchin'

THINKING INSIDE THE BOX
Why I Never Throw Out an Original Train Box

I recently added Lionel no. 16850 operating wind turbines to my O gauge layout. They look and work great, and visitors to my store like them a lot. However, I ran into a problem with the original boxes these accessories were packed in.

Over the years, I've accumulated many empty boxes from the stuff added to the layout. There are boxes from every train, building, accessory, vehicle, and carnival ride shoved under the table and crammed into cubby holes at the shop. With so much under the layout, I find it hard to go under it to work on wiring.

For good reason, then, I was about the crush the big boxes the wind turbines came in. Then a little voice in the back of my brain told me to stop.

That voice was reminding me of all the prewar and postwar trains I've bought throughout the years and how often I had wished the original owners had not discarded the original boxes. It pointed out how excited I had been when discovering a vintage item in like-new condition and with its great original box.

Those situations have never been particularly common. Years ago, kids and other hobbyists just didn't think of toy trains as future collectibles. That's the reason the boxes for many engines, cars, and accessories were discarded. Additionally, many of these boxes were made of "cheesy" material, especially the set boxes.

This brings me to today's discussion of the original boxes. There's a fire raging in the collecting of original prewar and postwar boxes of all manufacturers. I know many folks couldn't care less about the box, but some people like to have something that others do not have. That's why original boxes have become such hot items.

Many boxes are worth more than the trains they were made for. Boxes are graded, just as toy trains are. Special terms referring to stability and clarity are generally used to describe boxes. In addition, the Train Collectors Association has recently devised a numerical scale to rate component and set boxes.

I like to refer to boxes using my own descriptive terms. For example, boxes can be "mushy"—all there, yet weak. "Crisp" boxes are my favorites; they're like-new. The cleanest and most stable boxes are known as "bricks."

The most collectible boxes are set boxes, which held an entire outfit, and master cartons, which contained the engine and tender in their individual boxes.

Master cartons are very desirable and some are worth as much as or more than their original contents. Auctions often sell set boxes and master cartons separately from the engines and cars, getting more bidders to pay higher prices.

As usual, supply and demand rules the value of these paper treasures. I've seen people pay crazy prices for empty original cartons. They know that having the correct original box can double or triple the value of a desirable prewar or postwar train. Pride of ownership fuels the rise in prices for scarce boxes.

So what should I do with the boxes stored under my layout? I do have them on boards so air can get underneath them in case of any minor water problem. But it's getting to the point where I can't keep them all. Honestly, I have discarded many boxes for MTH and Lionel MPC starter sets that I broke up for individual sales.

What's a Lionel Pennsylvania Freight Flyer set box from 1990 worth? Not much—now! Who knows what will happen in the future? That is why folks have become more aware of the value of original boxes in the past 35 years. And why most trains produced these days stay with their original box.

Keep searchin'!

Finding the Magic
Never Forget the Joys of Vintage Toy Trains

February reminds me of one of the saddest days of my young life. I'm referring to the winter day in February 1959, when a plane crash killed three of my rock 'n' roll heroes: Buddy Holly, Richie Valens, and J.P. Richardson (known to the world as "The Big Bopper"). More than a decade later, Don McLean immortalized that tragedy in his classic song, *American Pie*, as "the day the music died."

Fifty years after the event, I used it as the basis of my Views From The Underground in the February 2009 issue of *Classic Toy Trains*. What I meant when I spoke about "the day the music died" in regard to toy trains related to how reissues changed the ways hobbyists collected Lionel trains from the modern era.

Specifically, I explained why I thought Lionel killed the collector's market in 1991 by producing the no. 18007 Southern Pacific 4-8-4 GS2 *Daylight* steam locomotive, a virtual twin to the no. 8307 SP GS4 Lionel had cataloged in 1983.

I would like to revisit that discussion, particularly in light of comments my fellow collectors have made and the time I've had to think about what happened.

In 1969, Lionel leased the rights to make and market its trains to General Mills, which reproduced many classics from the postwar era. Too bad those models lacked the quality of their predecessors. Things improved in the late 1970s and '80s, when new styles and road names were introduced. People started buying these new models under the assumption they were not going to be repeated in future years.

In other words, hobbyists acted as though once Lionel released an item the company would never make that model again. After all, this practice had been true with postwar classics, such as the Canadian Pacific streamlined passenger train. Wrong!

When Lionel Trains Inc. released the 18007 GS2 SP *Daylight* steam locomotive it was almost identical to the 8307 GS4 *Daylight*. Keep in mind, the latter 4-8-4 was the first new style of steam engine produced by General Mills that boasted increased significant value (from $400 to $2,000).

Readers of my February 2009 column pointed out that Lionel did remake some postwar trains back in the 1970s and early '80s. However, many of the "new style" and "new road names" did rise in value. As examples they mentioned the *Blue Comet*, the *Alton Special*, and the Chessie steam set, among others. I had focused on the *Daylight* steamer, which was remade in 1991 after it achieved the highest collector value.

That reissue caused some people to lose confidence in the collectibility of Lionel trains. They realized that once a toy train became popular it could be reproduced many times, like Christmas cookies, and would never become rare. That's not bad for the folks who did not own the initial production model.

I personally think toy trains are to be run and enjoyed. However, I have to admit I find collecting fever is very enjoyable, fulfilling, and expensive. It's human nature to desire, hunt for, and preserve something that very few other people possess.

That being said, I can state with 100 percent accuracy that no other original prewar or postwar trains will be produced since those years have gone. Therefore, that's the place to start if you want to collect something with assurance it won't be back.

As for you, who love to run trains for yourself and your family, let me say that trains are still a good personal investment in all the enjoyment they bring and can be passed on for generations.

So you see, the music did not really die.

Keep searchin'!

You Never Know Just What You'll Find
Toy Train Collections Provide Many Memories

During the early 1980s I advertised in newspapers around my home in western Pennsylvania for old toy trains. I kept what I wanted for my collection and sold the excess, usually at local and regional train shows. Shows were perfect for selling what I didn't want before I opened my store, the Underground Railroad Shoppe, in 1985.

There were many shows, and I traveled all over the Northeast to sell trains and accessories. Shows were held at firehalls, hotels, schools, and malls, usually starting on Friday evening and lasting through Sunday afternoon.

While setting up to sell my trains and accessories, I always put up a large sign indicating I bought old toys and trains. People who were at the mall often responded to my sign, and I would make an appointment to visit their home and look at their trains in the evenings after the mall closed.

Since I traveled long distances to these shows, it gave me a good chance to buy trains in areas where I would not otherwise get a chance to advertise.

Dealers told themselves that you never knew just what you were going to find on some of these evening buying trips. It was a thrill to enter a house or apartment to inspect the trains being offered for sale.

I always tried to screen the seller to see if the trains were something I would be interested in before I made a commitment to go to the house.

I bought many trains and toys on these home visits. Postwar Lionel and American Flyer were the most plentiful, but I also purchased prewar

Ives and Voltamp trains, Buddy-L trucks, and even Howard models from the early 20th century. Occasionally, there were scarce items and many were in great condition, so it was exciting to find these treasures. Every train and every seller had a story.

I could write many pages about the various trains I bought over that 35 years, but it is sufficient to say this has been a great life experience.

It was fun getting a chance to open up these treasure chests of Christmases past. Boxes labeled "Jimmy's Train" in crayon, old Christmas cards, gift tags, and 60-year-old newspapers added a sense of history, as did all the wonderful figures, buildings, vehicles, fences, and little mirrors used for lakes under the tree that I found in these boxes.

Many of the items I purchased were not valuable in a monetary sense. However, tons of memories poured out of every opened box.

It gave me an odd feeling to look down on items that were so personal to their former owners. I often wondered how folks could part with these memorable toys and electric trains.

I wish it had been possible to keep everything I discovered, but space and money prohibited that. I'm just thankful for what I was able to hold on to. I plan to enjoy every piece in my collection and pass it down to my family.

The chances to buy old trains have diminished from 35 years ago, when I would get two or three phone calls every day just in my area. These days, I end up buying collections of trains that were bought during the past 25 years.

Fortunately, I still get people walking into my store, eager to sell old trains that have been in storage since the 1950s. These are the nuggets that are still exciting to view. Boxes marked "Joey's Train" or just "Train" are invitations to travel back decades to a time when everything was good with the world, or at least we thought it was, and that's okay with me.

Keep searchin'!

Clowns, Hobos, and Trains
The Appeal of Circuses and Hobo Camps on Layouts

As a boy growing up in western Pennsylvania during the 1940s and '50s, one of the most memorable events in my life was the arrival of a circus in my hometown. Circuses traveled by rail in those days, and a circus train was colorful and bigger than life. The early circus trains were pulled by steam locomotives and contained decorative boxcars, passenger coaches, and flatcars loaded with wagons that carried wild animals.

My buddies and I would arrive early in the morning to see the great train pull in at the local rail yard. We loved seeing a combination of two of our favorite things in life: trains and the circus.

Each railcar was methodically unloaded by workers. Horse-drawn wagons carrying the cages were lined up, along with many of the clowns and circus performers. Sometimes a band would be in the parade; during other years, cars equipped with loud speakers provided wonderful circus music.

The parade would march through town to a large baseball field, where workers would set up the tents. We kids would follow them to the field. Sometimes we were hired to run errands in exchange for free tickets for the circus. It was a thrill just to be around what was called "the greatest show on earth."

My love for the circus is also displayed in the O gauge layout built at my store, the Underground Railroad Shoppe, located in New Castle,

Pa. I have a large amusement park, a small carnival, and a circus train all integrated with the scenery and structures.

Unfortunately, as other modelers can probably tell, it's hard to display a full circus since the tent is large and much of the action is covered. I do have an outdoor ring in my amusement park that shows various circus performers and clowns. The amusement park and the circus are very popular with the people who visit my store each year.

That's not all. My own collection includes an American Flyer circus train. The S gauge set cataloged by the A.C. Gilbert Co. in 1950-51 (no. 5002T) train included a steam locomotive and tender, one coach, and two flatcars with animal cages. I added two more coaches and six flatcars to create a long and impressive train.

Many of you will recall how K-Line was starting to produce beautiful O gauge circus trains and accessories. I wish someone would continue bringing out similar train products. Frankly, I believe that every toy train layout could use a nice circus on it.

Why do I write that? Because I've always loved the people who traveled with the circuses and carnivals that came through my hometown. They provided a peek at another life with a strange taste of freedom my friends and I knew we would never have.

Hobos were also a part of this rambling section of our society that would blow into our lives over the rails. Trains provided transportation for a nomadic group of people who traveled from town to town. Those fellas would steal rides on trains and travel the country looking for odd jobs. Hobo camps along the tracks were common, with tramps eating, sleeping, and staying there until the next train came along.

During the Great Depression of the 1930s, hobo camps were common sights. Even if they're gone today, we can add a touch of realism to our layouts by re-creating a hobo camp. In fact, I have a few of them on my store's railroad. Each has a flickering campfire and guys sleeping on the ground with newspapers covering their faces.

There you have it: clowns, hobos, and trains, all part of our colorful past, and still part of our toy train hobby.

Keep searchin'!

CATALOGS FEED OUR LOVE OF TOY TRAINS
Memories of Sears, American Flyer, and Other Paper

Growing up in the central part of Pennsylvania in the 1940s, my earliest memories tell me the Sears, Roebuck catalog was the first thing I would read when looking for ideas for Christmas gifts.

I can remember spending countless hours leafing through the thin pages of that catalog, where I discovered all the toys I wanted. Toys and trains, along with tools, sports equipment and anything else Mom or Dad needed could be found there.

In December of 1951, I received my first train catalog. A new American Flyer S Gauge catalog from the A.C. Gilbert Co. came with my first train. My family presented me with a no. 5003T steam passenger set, which included a no. 290 4-6-2 Pacific and tender pulling a pair of the no. 652 New Haven coaches in green and a matching no. 650 observation car.

Train catalogs became a big part of my young life. Each year I would get the new Flyer and Lionel catalogs and dream of all the trains I'd like. The beautiful colors and artwork made me drool every time that I turned a page. The train catalogs of the 1950s were the best ever. They rivaled the comic books and baseball cards I was collecting at that time.

I still look at those vintage catalogs. I do so for my own enjoyment and to help customers who walk into my store (the Underground Railroad Shoppe in New Castle, Pa.) and try to describe the childhood trains they no longer have.

The look on the faces of these sad customers is priceless when I find the exact set. They're shocked I have original catalogs depicting their first train. And they are absolutely thrilled! They have big smiles when we begin the search for the engines and cars to re-create their cherished sets.

Funny thing, these ecstatic customers want more than just their original sets. They also want the original catalogs that can document what they have.

This same thing is happening to customers who were children a generation later, in the 1970s and '80s. Catalogs from that part of the modern era provide the same avenue to launch searches for long-lost yet beloved toy trains. I have to be sure I can show them the catalogs they recall owning.

New parents who have reached their 40s are searching for trains like those they had as kids. Yes, it seems like the wheel just keeps turning!

Much as I love catalogs, I have two problems with current ones.

First, toy train manufacturers issue too many catalogs each year. They should do what Lionel and Gilbert did during the postwar era and put out just one catalog annually for each scale of train they produce. Many trains and accessories are repeated in each volume. Also, multiple catalogs cost a bunch of money to produce, and the paper required doesn't make them environmentally friendly.

Second, manufacturers should produce all the trains illustrated in their catalogs. Doing so would reduce a lot of frustration for customers, who order products yet never get them before the end of the catalog year.

Putting these two problems with current catalogs aside, it should be plain to that I still love catalogs and look forward to the new ones. But my old catalogs hold a special place in my heart and always will.

Keep searchin'!

THE VALUE OF A CHIP
Tiny Imperfections Affect What a Model is Worth

I've been doing some thinking about "chips." But what kind am I referring to?

Go to Las Vegas and you'll hear folks talking about chips all the time. They're focusing on gaming chips, which can vary in value from $5 to $5,000 each.

The chips on my mind relate to toy trains. Here again, though, that term can have different meanings, depending on whom you're talking with.

Chips can refer to electronics components. They can be a circuit on a tiny semi-conductor in the boards that operate the latest locomotives from Lionel, MTH, and others.

No, the chips that have lately been my concern bring us back to the world of toy train collecting. When I started to collect back in the 1970s, hobbyists were concerned about chips on the original paint of prewar and postwar locomotives and cars.

Every chip hurt the *monetary* value of a vintage item. The upside of a well-used train with lots of chips is that someone had a lot of fun with that model. Chips mean a youngster played with it for many hours.

But chips have a negative impact on a train's monetary value. A vintage model would have the highest value if there were no chips on the original paint. In that case, what I refer to when grading trains as the "sheen" would be perfect and pristine.

I don't always agree with the rating scales collectors are currently using. "Mint," "Like New," and so forth are words we rely on to describe conditions of trains; however, there are subtle yet important variations in each of these grading categories.

A scale that rates the condition of models between 1 and 10 also has variations for each number. It's difficult to get hobbyists to agree on these categories. Some collectors and dealers are said to be "strict graders," while others take a looser approach.

In my opinion, the only grade that matters is the selling (not the asking) price of an item. For example, a Lionel no. 736 Berkshire steamer that sells for $500 would, in my view, grade above the same model fetching $125. The difference in the selling prices represents the grading disparity.

The grading you can't dispute is that of an item that's never been run and is new-in-the-box or a model sealed in its original box. Trains of that nature vary in the price people will pay for them, so the grading is not in question.

Going back to my idea of the sheen of an original prewar or postwar train, the concept is hard to explain. But I can assure you I know it when I see it.

There's nothing better than examining a postwar piece in its original crisp box, wrapped in stiff brown paper from the manufacturer, and seeing sheen that looks as though it was made yesterday. The item has an unmistakable sparkle or luster all its own. You know it was hardly used before being carefully put away. Sometimes I'm checking out an engine, freight car, or accessory that hasn't been reopened for 50 years or more.

There are times when even these "like new" trains have a few chips on them. The paint may have been faulty when the item was produced, or it may have been bumped in storage. Each chip does deter from the value.

Collectors who pay big money for pristine models will reject anything that has chips. Nevertheless, the final selling price of such an item—or any train —will determine the grade better than any reference book.

Finally, let me remind you there are still other kinds of chips. My favorites are homemade potato chips, which always taste better with a glass of ice-cold brew!

Keep searchin'!

THE BEST COMBINATION
We Love Our Music as Much as We Do Our Trains

Listen to my story of a love for rock music and toy trains and see if it doesn't fit your life.

I bought my first 45-rpm record in 1957—*At The Hop* by Danny and The Juniors. My older sister had given me a small brown RCA 45-rpm record player, so I had no problem spinning my new platter. That phonograph had a large spindle with a red top.

Prior to that, I would listen to 78-rpm records on the big wooden Victrola in the living room of my family's home. I loved playing tunes from the 1940s and early '50s on that Victrola, I listened to the big bands, and first heard a young singer by the name of Frank Sinatra on a 78-rpm record. I enjoyed the popular music of that era and still do.

But then I got my own record player, which I set up in my bedroom to play the music disc jockeys were calling "rock 'n' roll." That was a great thing for a kid in the eighth grade. Soon I was buying more records, including what is still my favorite song—*In the Still of the Night* by the Five Satins. Instead of chasing trains anymore, my buddies and I were chasing something else…that's right, girls!

Rather than spend my money on American Flyer cars and accessories, I was saving up for a set of drums. I learned to play and began singing. With those same pals, I formed bands to play rock 'n' roll, especially doo-wop songs. One garage band was called the Sky Rockets, another was the Jazzmen. We spent our extra money on records and instruments.

138

I never lost my love of early rock 'n' roll. At my home you'll see lots of musical memorabilia from those years. Start with an original Seeburg jukebox and a stack of old 45-rpm records. Then check out the vintage Coca-Cola vending machine that is completely refurbished (you can still get a Coke for 10 cents in my house!).

During those years in high school, trains took a backseat. My family's tree always had my train around it when it was put up during the Christmas season. However, I admit that many of those holidays no longer included countless hours playing with trains. Sometimes the train ran only once or twice when we put up the tree.

Look, like many of you I was too busy with music or other activities. The old Flyer train ceased to be put under the tree when I no longer lived at home with my parents. Then I packed away the trains, along with my 45-rpm records and baseball cards. Thanks go to my mom for saving all those goodies from my youth.

Later, when I was married and my wife, Marcia, and I had our own home, that love of trains returned with a vengeance. My memories exploded into a fury of desire to re-create the years when I gleaned so much enjoyment from those little electric toys. That's what I call "the magic of toy trains." I now have more trains than I had ever dreamed of.

Yes, I do, and I still do love rock 'n' roll. Music provided a good place for me during my younger years. I never miss a chance to get together with my old friends or anyone else who wants to play rock 'n' roll or sing doo-wop songs. I forget many things these days, but I still remember all the lyrics to those old songs. I guess it's because they are sandwiched between many good times and wonderful years.

Frankie Lymon and The Teenagers sang, *Why Do Fools Fall in Love?* I know why fools such as I fall for rock 'n' roll and toy trains.

They bring back the romance of times gone by. See whether my story isn't yours and feel free to share your memories.

Keep searchin'

Back to the Future
A New Direction for Today's Starter Sets

I recently purchased a box filled with a vintage electric train set that someone brought into my store, The Underground Railroad Shoppe, located in New Castle, Pa. The trains belonged to the father of the man who sold them to me.

Inside that dusty carton I discovered the components of a Lionel O-27 set cataloged in 1948—the no. 1427WS.

Upon examining the box of trains, I found the trains were in pristine condition. I was especially amazed at the quality of the vintage steam locomotive. It was a no. 2026 2-6-2 steamer equipped with a die-cast metal body and handrails, a working headlight, puffing smoke, and nickel-rimmed drive wheels. The no. 6466WX tender had handrails, a great-sounding whistle, and die-cast metal trucks rear coupler.

The freight set also included nos. 6454 New York Central boxcar, 6465 Sunoco double-dome tank car, and 6257 Lionel Lines Southern Pacific-type caboose. All the cars were constructed using heavy-duty plastic and came with metal bases on which were mounted heavy die-cast metal trucks and couplers.

The 60-year-old outfit looked as if someone had bought it new this year. It had all the components to start kids between 5 and 10 years of age into the hobby for the rest of their life. And it got me thinking about how starter sets have changed over the years.

When I opened The Underground Railroad Shoppe in 1985, I couldn't help being disappointed in the new starter sets that were available at that time. Many of them included plastic DC locomotives. Those sets that did come with a lightweight die-cast metal engine tended to have a 4-4-2 steamer with a rubber traction tire on one drive wheel powered by a small can-style motor. The traction tires often came loose and had to be replaced by my staff.

The rolling stock was also cheaply constructed of light plastic with plastic trucks and couplers. The couplers often malfunctioned due to the flimsy plastic tab that operated them. The most disappointing thing was that the steam locomotives in the starter sets of that era had no whistle!

Lionel, to its credit, did try to interest kids by releasing starter "play sets" in the late 1970s and '80s. They included the nos. 1860 and 1862 Workin' on the Railroad sets (cataloged in 1978), 1053 James Gang western set (1980), L.A.S.E.R. (1981-82), 1254 Black Cave Flyer (1982), and 1355 Commando Assault Train (1983-84).

Many of those Lionel sets included colorful accessories, which gave them lots of play value. Unfortunately, they were made of flimsy, lightweight plastic that a child easily broke.

Looking at what's on the market today, I find that starter sets have improved. For example, all the locomotives now have a whistle or a horn.

Even so, I still prefer the older engines. When I hold in one hand Lionel's 0-8-0 steam engine (the motive power for most of its new starter sets) and that vintage Lionel 2026 in my other hand, I like the heft of the older locomotive.

I would encourage today's manufacturers to revisit those Lionel play sets of the 1970s and '80s, only this time they should make them more durable and include at least one operating car. Also, the trucks and couplers on the cars should be sturdy and trouble free. Finally, a young child should be able to activate sounds with ease.

This is the future of the hobby. We can go back to the future and learn a lot.

Keep searchin'!

2013

Lunch Money
How to Spend Your Train Dollars in the New Year

Happy New Year! The new year of 2013 will soon be here. You know what that means—many of us will be contemplating resolutions to help us improve during the coming year. You make them regarding how to spend your free time and what to do to make yourself healthier. Here are two resolutions related to our favorite hobby of toy trains— ideas on how to spend your train dollars wisely in 2013.

First, make an updated inventory list of the trains and accessories you own. For some of you, that involves updating an inventory you have. For most of you, that means making your initial attempt at keeping track of what you have.

Second, purchase insurance for your collection. If you have insurance, then update your policy to reflect changes in the toy train market. If you have never bought insurance for your collectible trains, this is the perfect time to learn what you need and take this smart and necessary plunge.

Insurance is important to have for your train collection, no matter what size it is, and you want the proper amount of coverage. Nearly all the firms that insure trains require pictures of what you own and an accurate and up-to-date inventory of what you have bought, inherited, traded for, and more.

The inventory should be current and realistic. Each item ought to be properly graded and priced at what it is worth in today's market. The initial cost of a train has nothing to do with its current price. Maintaining old and unrealistic prices can only hurt in any type of claim or future reference, so keep the values up to date.

How do you determine the value of your trains? Purchase the most current edition of the *Greenberg Pocket Price Guides* put out by Kalmbach Publishing Co. The guide to Lionel trains is updated and expanded every year. The guide to American Flyer and other S gauge brands is improved every other year; the guide to Marx is done less frequently.

In cases of theft, fire, or other damage to the trains, insurance companies may verify the current value. Such firms and lawyers have hired me to do that. It is important to have accurate prices of what you own. Overinflating the value of your trains is not a good idea. It is more expensive, and you may get only the current replacement cost.

I can tell you it's difficult to buy trains from people who have an overinflated train list plus little knowledge about the current toy train market. On the other hand, families are thrilled when Dad's prewar or postwar collection is worth significantly more than they dreamed. I am pleased to pay a widow a large sum of money for those trains. It is like Pop left Mom a nice, unexpected gift from beyond.

It's interesting to see how differently children can react to selling their father's train collection. Some of these men and women don't want to sell it at any price. What I offer is only "lunch money" to them. You can't put a price on emotions connected to toy trains.

Occasionally, the surviving family members seem interested in getting the highest buck for Dad's treasures. I encourage them to keep them in "the family."

There are times when some of the kids do keep the trains. They get them clean and running and become collectors and operators. I like to see the memory live on.

We love our trains, so its good to protect them for our families and ourselves. An inventory and insurance are essential.

Keep searchin'!

MAGIC CARPETS MADE OF STEEL—PART 1
Never Overlook VINTAGE Toy Train Track— or Underestimate its Importance

The name of a radio show I created and hosted at a local station on Saturday mornings during the holiday season was called "Train of Thought." For six weeks, I talked with guests and callers about toy trains and the hobby of model railroading. The program proved to be popular during the 10 years that it ran, but then the station changed its format and canceled the show. I really miss it.

Naturally, the show needed a memorable and entertaining theme song, one that I could play at the beginning and the end of each program. I chose what remains my all-time favorite railroad pop song, "The City of New Orleans," which was written by the late Steve Goodman and sung by Arlo Guthrie. (Willie Nelson also did a great version.)

You'll remember the song presents a nostalgic view of the *City of New Orleans*, the Illinois Central passenger train that traveled between Chicago and New Orleans.

Steve Goodman wrote some memorable lyrics. I especially liked the line in the song that described the streamlined train traveling on a "magic carpet made of steel."

Too often, whether we're thinking of full-size or miniature trains, we forget all about the track. That's too bad because, as we all know, tracks tie everything together. They make it possible for locomotives to speed across layouts, with freight or passenger cars in tow.

Surprisingly, considering how important track systems are, they remained all but unchanged for decades in toy train circles. You had three-rail tubular track made of steel for Lionel's Standard gauge trains plus its smaller O and O-27 models. T-Rail sections made their debut in the late 1930s for advanced modelers, but didn't return after World War II.

Meanwhile, S gauge enthusiasts were depending on the two-rail straights and curves sold by the A.C. Gilbert Co. for its American Flyer line. Except for the absence of a center rail, those steel sections with ties at the ends and the middle were like Lionel's.

About the only significant exceptions to what was available was Lionel's effort at greater realism with Super O track between 1957 and 1965 and Gilbert's flimsy Pikemaster track in 1965 and '66. Not many hobbyists took advantage of GarGraves flextrack for their O gauge layouts, although that product was always available.

When I opened my toy train store, the Underground Railroad Shoppe in New Castle, Pa., in 1985, my inventory hardly differed from what I might have sold 30 years earlier. I stocked new O-27 and O gauge straights, curves, and switches from Lionel. K-Line offered items that were all but identical. As for S gauge, Gilbert was gone but K-Line made wide-radius track, which was a great improvement for Flyer operators.

Of course, I also carried bundles of clean, rust-free used track. They flew off the shelf, as did refurbished American Flyer and Lionel manual and remote-controlled switches. People would also buy track in any shape and clean it if the price was right.

Times have sure changed since I got started – and generally, for the better! But that is my subject for the next issue of *Classic Toy Trains*. See you then!

Keep searchin'!

Magic Carpets Made of Steel—Part 2
Great Systems of O and S Gauge Track
Fill the Current Toy Train Market

In the February issue of *Classic Toy Trains*, I focused on what I consider one of the most important and overlooked areas of the hobby—track.

For many years, layout builders depended on vintage track or at least systems that had scarcely changed from the postwar era. Today, though, we are fortunate to have new and terrific systems of O and S gauge track to consider when designing a layout. Manufacturers have developed great systems, regardless of whether someone is building a realistic or a traditional "toy-rail" layout. One more reason this is the best time to be in the hobby.

Looking back to 1986, when I started building an O gauge layout in my store (the Underground Railroad Shoppe in New Castle, Pa.), I didn't have much to choose from. If I wanted realism, then it was GarGraves flextrack with its blackened center rail. If I wanted a vintage look, then it was tubular track. And I opted for the latter, going with Lionel sections: 10- and 40-inch-long straights and curves ranging from O-31 to O-42 to O-72.

When MTH Electric Trains introduced its RealTrax O gauge system, I was excited. It featured solid brass rails mounted on a nicely textured gray plastic roadbed. The first modern era track system to include a roadbed, RealTrax was a great addition to the model train hobby.

Some operators felt the blackened center rail did not conduct electricity efficiently and sanded that rail. Unfortunately for those enthusiasts, their modification diminished the realistic look of the track. Also, the Magne-Traction found on some Lionel locomotives didn't function on brass rails.

Not to be outdone by its chief rival, Lionel came out with a new system called FasTrack (steel tubular track installed on a textured plastic roadbed). I liked the large pins connecting each section, along with the clip fastening the track on the underside of the roadbed. FasTrack sections stay together for people using it for layouts resting on carpet and running around a Christmas tree.

Since MTH and Lionel began putting these systems in all of their new ready-to-run train sets, the demand for O-27 and O gauge tubular track—new or old—has decreased at my store. Also dampening demand are ScaleTrax, the realistic system developed by MTH to compete with GarGraves, and 21st Century Track, produced by Atlas for the O gauge market.

Still other outstanding O gauge items are the turnouts and crossovers from Ross Custom Switches and GarGraves (in business since the late prewar period).

Hobbyists planning S gauge layouts no longer need to search for vintage American Flyer track. American Models, Lionel, and S-Helper Service raised the bar significantly when it came to appearance and conductivity of S gauge track.

My comments don't exhaust everything that's happened with O and S gauge track in recent years. I could write pages on all the new innovations and attention that leading manufacturers have given to their toy train track systems. Suffice it to say that the "magic of toy trains" is made possible, as it always was, by the "magic carpets made of steel."

Keep searchin'!

iPHONIA
We Can Benefit by Using Cell Phones at Train Shows

Let's talk seriously about cell phones and their place at train shows large and small around the country. These devices, increasingly inexpensive and commonplace, have transformed life in America. And they have a useful place for hobbyists attending shows. Yet for reasons no longer relevant, cell phones have been prohibited from many of the train meets I have attended as a consumer or an exhibitor.

When cell phones began to appear in the late 1970s, they were very expensive. As a consequence, only folks with a lot of money were able to buy them.

The toy train clubs and associations that managed the shows concluded that the small number of people able to obtain cell phones would have a distinct buying advantage by communicating with their buddies in other halls to get the best buys. They also claimed that cell phones interfered with the two-way radios officials used to communicate with each other during the shows. Therefore, they banned cell phones.

Keep in mind that cameras also are not allowed at many meets. The rationale is that banning them (including phones that can take pictures) protects members from having photos taken of their trains by dishonest individuals who may plan to steal them.

These rules are still in force throughout the country. I think the time is right for club officers to revisit these regulations to be more in step with modern technology.

Today, it's difficult to find a person who does not own a cell phone. Prices for cell phones have fallen to the point that everyone in the hobby should be able to afford one.

The Bluetooth headset hangs on a guy's ear. It's hard to tell whether he's using it as a phone or walking around talking to himself!

At the same time, most cell phones are small and also serve as a camera. It's hard to detect a person using his or her cell phone as a camera. Needless to say, it's hard to enforce cell phone and camera prohibition.

I believe cell phones are useful and positive tools for communication. They add convenience and provide extra safety for everyone using them. Let's not prohibit them!

However, many folks have taken all the new communications tools to another level of use in society. I'm referring to iPhones, Blackberries, and devices for texting.

Young people can seem obsessed with them. When my grandchildren visit, I see only the tops of their heads because they continually look into one of their palms as they operate some handheld phone. Of course, adults can also use these devices to an extreme. The folks who text or talk while driving their cars range in age from teens to seniors.

What about yours truly? I do have a cell phone; I do not have an iPhone or a Blackberry. I don't text. I am not on Facebook, and I don't tweet; in fact, I'm not even sure what that is! I live by the philosophy that everything is good in moderation.

That approach applies to cell phones, which is why they should be allowed at shows. I'm excited by the possibility of these devices being used to access and operate some of the latest toy trains. Manufacturers believe, as I do, that new technology can and should blend with the train hobby and enhance our enjoyment of it.

The train world will adapt to this new obsession that I call "iPhonia." I hope that the individuals in charge of our favorite meets will keep that point in mind. We must try to extract all the good that this new technology can offer and combine it with a lot of the old ideas that have ably served all of us in the world's greatest hobby for many years.

Keep searchin'!

LIGHTS, CAMERA, ACTION!
Getting a Layout Ready for Filming

I had the privilege of working with two of the best toy train journalists around: Roger Carp, a senior editor at *Classic Toy Trains* magazine, and Tom McComas, the owner of TM Books & Video.

Roger traveled to my store, the Underground Railroad Shoppe in New Castle, Pa., because CTT will be featuring the O gauge layout there in an upcoming issue. Tom showed up to produce a video on my business. Both experiences were interesting, especially because everything I did to prepare the layout should be done by anyone who has a model railroad.

The CTT story began with phone conversations between Roger and me as well as with photographer Dennis Brennan. We discussed the visit and all the areas to be covered, including how I entered the toy train hobby, planned my retail operation, and designed and constructed the layout. I enjoyed thinking about my years in the hobby and recommend you review yours.

Preparation for the photo shoot included cleaning everything that would be in the pictures—no dust or cobwebs allowed. The effort took a few nights and involved focusing on every square foot of my layout. I had to clean each vehicle and make sure all the figures were upright. Thousands of lights were checked to ensure they were in working order. I wanted trains to be running smoothly, so I cleaned the track and checked the electrical connections, fixing anything I had to.

All of that turned out to be quite a job. Remember, my O gauge layout is 25 years old, and I incorporate cool changes in the scenes every holiday season.

Even so, the process of preparing and checking over the layout was a valuable and worthwhile one. I suggest every one of you with a layout, no matter how new or old it is and regardless of its size and complexity, set aside some time on a regular basis to do the same thing. You may not be hosting a magazine editor or a video producer, but you'll want your railroad looking its best and running smoothly whenever a guest, neighbor, friend, or family member sees it.

Dennis meticulously set up the lights and the camera for each shot Roger and he planned with me. And that was a real challenge at times because the layout consumes most of the space in the room, with only a 5-foot-wide path around the table. It was difficult to get the lighting equipment and camera where necessary for a few photos.

Still, Roger and Dennis staged every picture to give CTT readers the best view of that particular scene. Different trains were used for each photo.

Soon after CTT visited, Tom McComas arrived with associate producer and cameraman Joe Stachler. These projects were in the planning stages for years, yet both occurred within the same month.

Tom provided a lot of entertainment when he interviewed me using my puppet, "Vinnie Boombatz." We talked about toy trains, and I shared several amusing stories and nuggets of hobby wisdom!

The result was a 40-minute video you'll enjoy. As noted on the cover, "All proceeds from the sale of this DVD go to Lou's favorite charity: The Palumbo Institute for Homeless Toy Train Collectors." Just kidding— Tom has quite a sense of humor!

The train hobby is lucky to have Tom McComas and Roger Carp, as they continue to provide great stories and videos related to the enjoyment of toy trains.

I'm fortunate to have Roger and Tom as associates in the business and as good friends. I'll continue to share my stories with you and as always, I will…

Keep searchin'

WORKING ON THE RAILROAD
The Memories that Inspire a Love for Toy Trains

So many of the toy train collectors and operators I meet at my store, the Underground Railroad Shoppe in New Castle, Pa., become regular customers and get around to telling me how memories inspire their love of toy trains. Many of them talk about building American Flyer or Lionel layouts with their father back in the post-World War II era.

The memories nurturing my love of all toy trains also originated then and remind me of my father. Unlike the recollections my customers share of old miniature trains, however, mine touch on full-size railroading. Dad worked for the Pennsylvania RR in the western part of the Keystone State, and I often assisted him.

It always seemed like it was a cold winter evening when Dad would get a call from his boss. Many times it was a Saturday night, while we were watching *Gunsmoke* or *Have Gun—Will Travel*, when Dad would have to inspect a train due to depart.

Dad was a car inspector for the Pennsylvania RR at New Castle Yard. One of his assignments was to inspect each freight train before it started on a journey to a new destination. Trains typically consisted of coal hoppers, boxcars, gondolas, and tankers.

I always liked the weekend evening calls because Dad would take me along to assist him. And Dad liked the calls for a simple yet intelligent reason.

Let me put it this way: That was the first time I ever heard the phrase, "Time and a half." Understand?

Dad and I would arrive at the yard where the train was ready to leave within hours. Being in my early teens, I was able to help him carry some of the equipment and hold the lantern, as it was usually dark when we got these calls. I know that today's rules would prohibit me from going with my father, but circumstances were different back in the mid-1950s, which is why I'm happy to have had those experiences then.

My father and I would start at the supply shed where he kept the tools and materials for the job. The trains were usually over a mile long, and he would inspect the air hoses and journal boxes on each car. The journal boxes were metal boxes located at the end of the axle of each car. A heavy steel lid was opened to see if the box was filled with a shredded heavy cotton fiber soaked in oil. If the box was low or empty, we would refill it.

Naturally, the two of us had to walk the entire length of the train, checking both sides of the freight cars. To be honest, that long, long walk was not very much fun.

At the end of the train was the caboose, and my favorite thing was to check it. The caboose was a magical car, complete with bedding (black leather cushions), cooking materials, and a potbelly stove. It's too bad railroads no longer put a caboose on each train. I know that practice was ended for economical reasons, but an end-of-train device (EOT) will never replace a caboose on my O gauge layout.

I liked to climb up into the cupola, where there were cushions to lay down, and look out the windows. Sometimes the locomotive could be seen from the windows.

Dad and I made sure each caboose had the needed supplies. Cushions were checked and replaced if damaged. Flares, flags, kerosene lanterns, work rags, and warning caps were some of the items supplied.

The long and tiring evening would end hours later with a cup of hot coffee in the caboose and many happy memories for me. That's why my love for trains stems back to all of those years growing up with my dad and the railroad—a full-size one. They are relived every time I see and use the model trains that we have to enjoy in this hobby.

Keep searchin'!

THE PAPER CHASE
The Pleasures of Collecting Vintage Toy Train Catalogs

I recently acquired a great collection of Lionel catalogs from the years 1945 to 1999. Vintage catalogs were hot items in the 1970s and '80s, when the passion for collecting postwar trains and accessories was exploding. Just about every train show I attended had several vendors who were peddling old Lionel catalogs from the pre- and post-World War II periods.

I felt the same enjoyment chasing after catalogs as I did hunting for vintage toy trains. Most of all, I liked the catalogs issued between 1946 and 1959. If I had to choose my favorite catalog from those years, well, it would really be a tough decision.

I like the trains Lionel offered in its catalog for 1950, but my favorite cover was on the consumer catalog for 1952. It showed a lad looking over a bridge with a no. 624 Chesapeake & Ohio NW2 diesel switcher pulling a freight train across that massive structure. There are six steam and diesel locomotives under the bridge, all of which were quite impressive when shown lined up next to each other.

My favorite American Flyer catalog is still the one from 1950. The cover features a boy and his friends sitting on cellar steps looking in amazement at a beautiful American Flyer layout. The S gauge railroad had six trains running as well as many neat operating accessories. There were also four large Erector set items.

I liked that Flyer catalog best because it illustrated and described the first train set given to me, the no. 5003T Pacific Fast Passenger set with a no. 290 New Haven 4-6-2 steam locomotive and tender heading three New Haven-style cars.

Every time I add a catalog to my collection, I read it from cover to cover when I get home. The artwork in those "wish books" transfers me back to the years when they were first produced. If you've never read an old toy train catalog, regardless of the manufacturer, take the time! They are choice!

The man who put together the collection of catalogs I purchased was meticulous. Most of the catalogs are in mint condition, and all the others are like new. He slid the catalogs into heavy plastic pages with a piece of cardboard support. They were then put into large binders for safekeeping.

I think the catalogs released between 1946 and 1959 boasted the finest artwork and the most magnificent colors. Those issued in the 1960s lacked much of that beauty. By then, of course, both Gilbert and Lionel were struggling financially. The catalogs those firms put out later in the '60s reflected their efforts to cut costs.

Lionel has made attempts in recent years to capture the magic of the old catalogs. Sorry to say, I don't think catalogs will ever be the same as those from the golden years of the 1950s, especially when many extra ones were put out in the 1970s, '80s, and '90s.

Don't get me wrong, however. I still enjoy every new catalog introduced each year. Flipping through them always sparks my interest in the latest offerings, even though I think too many catalogs are put out each year. Yet I get one of each catalog and add them to boxes of bound volumes. I often refer to more recent catalogs to identify trains I purchase. They are helpful as reference sources—but nothing else.

The old catalogs are different. Whenever I pick up one from the 1950s I end up reading the whole thing. It reminds me of when I am channel surfing on TV and come across *The Godfather* in progress. Yep, I end up watching the entire film to the end.

You just have to love vintage toy train catalogs and *The Godfather*.

Keep searchin'!

THE FUN HOUSE
Every Day is Special When You Own a Toy Train Store

Every time I tell my wife I'm going to the train store I own, she says, "You're not going to work; you're going to play with your friends."

I guess she's right! I love spending time at "The Fun House"—the Underground Railroad Shoppe—the store I own in New Castle, Pa. (You can read about my business and the O gauge layout you can visit there by turning to page 57 of this issue.)

I do have a lot of fun while buying, selling, repairing, and talking about toy trains. Regular customers and many good friends visit the store, but we also get a lot of people—individuals and families—who are just passing through the part of western Pennsylvania where it's located. No surprise to tell you the number of visitors has increased steadily since I began writing this column for *Classic Toy Trains* in November 2007.

My store, like every model train shop, is a place where customers share ideas about the hobby. Spirited conversations revolve around topics of importance, including S gauge versus O, MTH versus Lionel, FasTrack or tubular track, command control or conventional, and collecting or operating.

I also have strong opinions on different issues. Many times, however, I hold back my feelings so I don't offend my customers.

My dad always told me that when it comes to business, "You never get mad at money." I've tried to remember that advice and recommend other dealers do the same.

One of the more popular subjects brought up by the gang is the status of the toy train market. Guys young and old are always trying to analyze the direction the hobby is taking related to the value of their vintage and contemporary sets and models.

I listen courteously and ask the same question: "Why did you buy your trains?"

Most of the time, the consensus is customers bought their Lionel, American Flyer, MTH, or other brand for the enjoyment of collecting, displaying, and operating them.

"That," I respond, "is the value of your trains. Whatever money you get for them when they're sold is all profit!" Needless to say, the fierce discussions never end there.

Less heated are the ideas folks share about constructing layouts as well as some favorite tricks and techniques for restoring or repairing locomotives and cars.

The latest products always lead to fascinating discussions. Everyone seems to have an opinion or two on what manufacturers are doing right and wrong. Ideas of what they should be producing end up getting added to the mix.

The Underground Railroad Shoppe tends to be busiest between Thanksgiving and New Year's Day. I don't have as much time to talk with the people who stop by. That's okay because most of them want to check out the O gauge layout and see what changes I've made to it in recent months.

After the holidays, what I call the "hot stove" season for toy trains starts. In baseball that term refers to the winter months, when guys sit around a potbelly stove and "chew the fat" before the upcoming season begins. For toy train lovers, the "hot stove" season consists of the nine months between February and October. That's when we talk.

So you see, I do enjoy coming to "The Fun House." I guess Marcia is right when she says I'm going to work to play with my friends. The great guys in the train hobby are like a bunch of youngsters gabbing about what they did over summer vacation. We love reliving our early years when we discovered trains. Makes me realize how lucky I am to spend my days with people I really like and the hobby that enriches my life.

Keep searchin'!

A Wooden Station Gave My First Train Life
Fond Memories Can Come from Unexpected Places

I love telling the story of my first toy train. But it was something I got with it that left the best memories I have of that Christmas more than 60 years ago. You probably have a similar story about your childhood layout and a special piece on it.

Let's head to 1950. I finished first grade and learned to ride the J.C. Higgins two-wheel bicycle my folks bought me. Months later, Thanksgiving vacation was extended due to a 3½-foot snowfall. Snow was over my head!

I received my first train at Christmas. It was an American Flyer no. 5003T Pacific Fast Passenger set. That S gauge train had a no. 290 4-6-2 Pacific steamer and tender equipped with smoke and "choo-choo sound."

Smoke poured out of the engine as it pulled the three matching green-plastic New Haven heavyweight passenger cars around my imaginary world under the tree.

But only during the holiday season. Remember that back then houses were not spacious; every room was filled, and the cellars were small. No space for a large layout. Most trains owned by children were set up around the family Christmas tree. I was allowed to keep playing with my Flyer set for a few more weeks before I was nicely told to put it away for another year.

Like every kid, I hoped to expand my miniature empire. In fact, the first accessory I wanted was an American Flyer no. 589 Mystic station.

I first saw that sheet-metal structure in the Gilbert catalog for 1950 packed inside my train set's box.

I needed that station so my train would have a place to stop to pick up and deliver passengers. I showed the catalog to Dad and pointed out the Mystic station.

He said, "No problem." Frankly, I was surprised at how quickly my father had agreed to buy the station since I had already received all my Christmas gifts.

As I explained in the September 2013 *Classic Toy Trains*, Dad worked for the Pennsylvania RR. He and Mom also operated a small grocery store. She ran the store from day to day. Among the food sold was delicious Italian sausage Dad and I made. In our hometown of New Castle, Pa., people still talk about its taste.

Orange crates were always lying around the store. A day or two after my request for the Mystic station he presented me with a station he had made using the wood from an orange crate.

I was floored! Dad had made the station the right size and painted it red with a green roof. He made a bay window in the front out of a round piece of wood molding. Windows were painted on. He put "New Castle PA" on each end.

This was not what I had in mind when I had mentioned wanting a station, but I never let Dad know it. I put the station under the tree, where it remained every Christmas. Dad proudly pointed out the station when friends and relatives visited. I felt good about that. I still have the station today and display it every holiday season.

Recently, the station appeared in *Christmas Toy Train Stories*, a DVD from TM Books & Video. Producer Tom McComas recreated my first village under a Christmas tree. Watching the video brought back many fond memories. Every time I come across an American Flyer Mystic station I think of my dad and the wooden station. I'm lucky to have such warm and wonderful memories.

Merry Christmas and Happy Holidays.

Keep searchin'!

VIDEO OFFER

The Underground Railroad video is available! It contains many video shots of the layout and the shop.

In addition, it has new bonus footage of Lou's first American Flyer Christmas tree train.

The video can be ordered by email:
trainplum@yahoo.com

Or by calling the Underground Railroad Shoppe:
(724) 652-4912

$14.95
Free Shipping

74959734R00110

Made in the USA
Middletown, DE
01 June 2018